POWER TO CHOOSE

You have the power to choose self-esteem and self-confidence. You have the power to choose your attitudes, your goals in life and your motivation. This book will help you.

Haydn Sargent

DIRECT COMMISSION AUSTRALIAN MARKET

First published in October, 1989
by Boolarong Publications
12 Brookes Street, Bowen Hills, Q. 4006

Reprinted October, 1989
Reprinted September, 1992
Copyright © Haydn Sargent

National Library of Australia
Cataloguing-in-Publications data.

Sargent, Haydn, 1936 -
Power to choose.

Bibliography.
ISBN 0 7316 7606 8.

1. Success. 2. Motivation. 3. Self-confidence.
4. Self-respect. I. Title.

158

BOOLARONG PUBLICATIONS
12 Brookes Street, Bowen Hills, Brisbane. Qld 4006

Design, phototypesetting by Peter Iliffe and Graham Hitchins
Printed by Watson Ferguson & Company
Bound by Watson Ferguson & Company
Cover by Owen Davis.

There is no dress rehearsal in life.

This is the real thing.

Contents

Everybody Likes to Win

Everybody likes to win — and everybody can. However, when we think of winning, it's usually as a competition between ourselves and someone else. For many people that appears threatening.

Of course, we do often find ourselves in direct competition with someone else. Unfortunately, our society has become so competitive and we can become so fiercely aggressive that it can change our personalities and because we think that's the way it has to be, we run a mile rather than get into that style of competition.

I remember John Sieben, Australian Olympic gold medal winner, telling me of the atmosphere in the waiting area before an Olympic final. Some swimmers are so desperate to win that they resort to psychological warfare, trying to intimidate and harass other contestants with a whole range of subtle and not so subtle tactics, such as trying to outstare a nervous competitor or talking about a past swimming performance where they were better than others. In sport, in business, wherever there is competition, there are those who will try anything, from intimidation to cheating, to win.

During a visit to Canada our group travelled up Grouse Mountain, near Vancouver, and Sulphur Mountain, near Banff. Some of the people in the group were terrified of travelling in a cable car. After all, those cars did look rather inadequate dangling so far above the snow on what looked like a relatively thin cable. I believe the one way to overcome fear of that kind is to meet it head on. Each nervous person was partnered with a confident person and off we went. It wasn't easy for those who were afraid but they did it. They not only won over their fear, they also enjoyed that sweet sense of victory that comes to winners.

I believe that the biggest opportunity for winning is right there — in the challenge to overcome our own fears, take charge of our own lives and do something worthwhile with them. We don't have to live like victims. We can choose to win. We have the power to choose our own path through life.

While I was in Canada our coach driver stopped on the highway through the Rockies and pointed to a distant mountain, now called Mount Fox. It is named after a young man, Terry Fox. At just nineteen years of age, Terry was diagnosed as having cancer. His leg was amputated in an attempt to save his life. At twenty-one, with an artificial leg, Terry decided to run across Canada. His goal was to raise money for cancer research and to raise people's awareness of cancer. Terry never finished that heroic marathon. After 144 days and 5373 kilometres cancer invaded his lungs. He was forced to stop. Did he fail? Some people might say he failed. I wouldn't.

Terry Fox became a legend, not just in Canada but throughout the world. The Canadians came to love and admire him so much they re-named the mountain after him. Terry Fox was a winner, even though cancer took his young life and he never finished his run. Today, in over twenty countries around the world, Terry's dream is kept alive by millions of people who participate every year in the Terry Fox Run raising money for cancer research.

We live in an extremely competitive society and winning has become obsessively important to most of us. Some of us who claim we aren't interested in winning are probably trying to say that, because we get so sickened by the aggression of people wanting

3

to win, we'd rather back away from the competition. That's understandable but backing away from challenges can rob us of a real sense of achievement. There are lots of opportunities to win — not necessarily in conflict with another person but in challenging ourselves. We don't have to resort to aggression to beat others or to improve our own performance.

We need to rethink the words 'winning' and 'winner' and see them in their broadest and most exciting meanings. Life is a challenge — it's 'the game of your life' — and you can best develop yourself, your talents, abilities and gifts by accepting the challenge and competing with yourself to constantly improve on your personal best. In the process of doing that, you may well win in competition with others — they will become the motivation, a point of reference, not 'the enemy'. It doesn't have to be aggressive or unpleasant because your effort is always directed towards beating your previous best.

Taking up the challenge requires commitment and determination. We often admire other people for their single-minded sense of purpose as if they have a talent we don't or can't possess. I don't believe that spirit of dedication is reserved for a select few. Anyone can have it. If we want something badly enough, our desire, if it is strong enough, produces the sense of determined commitment to pursue our goal until we get it. Commitment and determination are perfectly natural and grow out of desire and conviction. A lot of people can't be bothered and that's OK if that's what they really want but they shouldn't wonder why life passes them by. You only get out what you put in.

I've never met anyone who didn't want to make a success of life — to win. But some people don't succeed. Why? I believe it's largely due to the fact that they don't realise they have the power to control their own lives.

You only get one shot at life.

So you may as well give it your best effort and make it as enjoyable, meaningful, adventurous, challenging and successful as you can.

This book will help you.

This Mysterious Act of Living

I've been a broadcaster and interviewer for over twenty years and I've been fortunate to meet and talk with some fascinating people, including royalty, prime ministers, premiers, cabinet ministers, film and TV stars, well-known recording artists, authors, professionals, the rich and the successful. I've also been fortunate to talk with lots of people who, while they are neither rich nor famous, they are successful, they are winning and they are achieving significant, worthwhile goals in their lives.

If I have learned anything as an interviewer and

broadcaster it's the useful skill of observation. In this book I want to share these observations with you, simply because I often see people struggling through life. They are underachieving, not realising their own potential and finding life a burden when it ought to be fun, stimulating and a real adventure.

You do not have to be rich or famous to be a winner — to be successful. If you make wealth a goal and you achieve it, that's a success. If you make fame a goal and achieve it, that's a success. However, you may choose to make a happy family life your goal. You may decide to make a worthwhile service to the community a goal. You may prefer to make the pursuit of excellence in a profession, trade or hobby your goal.

You don't have to be a celebrity or a well-known public figure to be successful. Plenty of quiet achievers in the world are enjoying their lives, pursuing their goals and making magnificent contributions to their community with a minimum of fuss and often no real recognition. They may be tradesmen, women at home, retired people, professionals or young people. They can be every bit as much winners as the people on the front pages receiving the awards.

> **To achieve what you set your sights on — that is winning! That is success!**

Og Mandino, author of *The Greatest Salesman Who*

Ever Lived, says, 'If you are going to play the game, you need to know the rules.' The following quote comes from another of his excellent books *The Greatest Success in the World*: "I am convinced," Zacchaeus said, "that life is just a game, here on Earth, a game where no one need be a loser, no matter what his plight or condition may be. I believe that everyone can enjoy the fruits of victory but I am equally as certain that, like all other games, *one cannot participate in this mysterious act of living with any hope of satisfaction unless one understands a few simple rules*."

Did anyone ever teach you the rules? Did any one of your teachers talk to you about things like self-confidence, self-esteem, choosing to adopt positive rather than negative attitudes, how to set goals, how to motivate yourself? No one did it for me, not even my parents who were just the most wonderful, loving and caring people. Once I had picked up Norman Vincent Peale's *The Power of Positive Thinking* I felt I had entered a whole new world of personal discovery. I am still reading and thinking about personal development. The day I lose interest in the topic I figure I'll be dead — if not in the body, then certainly from the neck up!

Owing to my interest in personal development, I've been analysing a lot of these success stories for over twenty years and they all appear to have a number of essential and basic qualities in common. I want to stress that they are essential qualities, for without them you'll be struggling to make a success of life. The five ingredients I am going to talk about in this book are all within everyone's reach. You don't have to be rich, educated or born in the right suburb to be able to take these five simple steps to winning.

Four of the five qualities are

> **self esteem** or what you think of yourself,
>
> **positive attitudes** in facing life and solving problems.
>
> **setting goals** to achieve what you want,
>
> **motivating** yourself.

The fifth one I'll leave until later in the book.

However, let me make this observation at the start: if you are going to set your sights on building a successful life, you have to make sure the foundations of your life, what you will build the rest of your life on, are right. For some people we may not be talking about repairing a few cracks. We could be talking about a complete rebuilding job, from the ground up. It's important to get the foundations of your life right otherwise everything you build on that could be shaky and you will have to start building all over again. So why not get it right, starting from the ground up? You may feel that is a radical step. But is it any worse than being unhappy and dissatisfied with yourself? The important thing is to start now.

I once overheard a conversation between two middle-aged women. One was saying how she wished she had gone to university and achieved her degree. The other asked her why she didn't go now, seeing her children were grown up and independent. 'It's too late,' was the reply, 'I'm forty-three.' The friend's response was spot on: 'If you start, you'll have your degree by forty-six. If you don't, you'll still be forty-six in three years' time and still complaining about your missed opportunity.'

This book is about making changes in your life so you can get the most out of your one shot at living.

The British actor Robert Morley tells the story about a man who bought a very expensive talking budgerigar. A week after he bought it, he was back in the pet shop complaining:

'You know that expensive talking budgerigar I bought off you last week? Well, it doesn't.'
'Oh, I forgot,' said the pet shop manager, 'he loves to sharpen his beak on a little cuttle fish before he gets going.'
So the man bought a year's supply. Next week, he's back again.
'He's still not talking.'
'My apologies,' said the pet shop man, 'he loves to ring a little bell before he starts talking.'
So the desperate owner buys a box of budgerigar bells.
You guessed it — a week later, he's back, most irate.

11

'That very expensive budgerigar you sold me hasn't said a word!'

'I forgot. I apologise,' said the salesman, 'he loves to run up a little ladder to the bell.'

So the frustrated owner of the very expensive, but non-talking budgerigar, now called Marcel Marceau, buys a hundred ladders.

Next week, the customer is back and not looking very happy at all.

The pet shop owner's curiosity got the better of him. 'Did he talk? Did he talk?' he asked.

'Yes,' said the sad looking owner, 'he spoke.'

'What did he say?' asked the pet shop man.

'Well, first he sharpened his beak on the cuttle fish. Then he ran up the ladders. Then he rang the bells and then he keeled over, flat on his back on the floor of the cage.'

'But I thought you said he spoke?' asked the pet shop man.

'He did,' said the sad looking owner of the now deceased, formerly expensive talking budgerigar. 'He said, "Didn't anybody say anything to you about bird seed?"'

> *Sometimes, when you are trying to solve problems, you have to get back to basics, to the essentials, to the beginning.*

I would like to take you back to the basics on the five fundamentals of success and winning because they are the foundation stones on which you are going to build your life.

'the unexamined life is not worth living'

It's All In
Your Head

Let's start with you. How do you feel about yourself? Do you feel good or bad? Do you like yourself? In other words, do you feel comfortable and at ease with yourself? If you find these questions hard to answer, let me put it this way: imagine there are two of you in the room — just the two of you and both identical in every way. Would you feel comfortable and at ease in the company of the 'other you'? Could you like him or her?

Unfortunately, a lot of people don't feel happy with themselves, which is a pity because you can't step out of being the person you are and go and live in another one, as if your 'person' is like an old jacket and you are in search of a more comfortable fit. Whatever you do in life, you can only do it with the person you were given on day one. However, you can make a lot of changes to the person you are — your appearance, health, physique and personality are changing all the time and you can do a lot to improve them. Albert Camus said: 'We continue to shape our personality all our life.' He was right. How many times have you known someone to undergo a complete change of personality to become bitter and resentful because of what has happened to them? On the other hand, can you recall someone changing for the better because of an experience in their lives? We can and do change.

Many people lack self-confidence. They don't have many good feelings about themselves at all. They often feel awkward, shy, self-conscious, inadequate and, because they are forever comparing themselves with others, they feel second class, even worthless. They convince themselves they are not as good as someone else because they are constantly feeling overshadowed by others. That attitude shows up in the work place, at home, school and in their social lives. That lack of self-confidence makes life a hell for many people. How about you?

Do you ever feel that way? If so, then here's the good news: you don't have to feel that way anymore if you don't want to! You can change and this book is dedicated to showing you how.

You may want to say, 'Yes, I feel OK about myself.' However, it's my observation that we are often reluctant to say yes to the idea of actually liking ourselves because we've been misled into thinking it's wrong to do so. Our society tends to look down on people who like themselves. When we were at school, we ridiculed someone for 'loving himself', for being too self-centred. It wasn't humble. But *liking yourself is essential to life.* If you think about it, liking yourself is essential to survival. Liking yourself doesn't mean you close your eyes to your own weaknesses and shortcomings. It doesn't mean you begin thinking you are perfect.

In a book called *The Art of Loving*, psychiatrist Eric Fromm says the idea expressed in the well-known phrase from the Bible 'love your neighbour as yourself' implies that respect for yourself, your own integrity, uniqueness and love for and understanding of yourself, cannot be separated from respect, love and understanding for other people. In other words, love for myself is connected with my love for any other person. Maybe that explains why some people find it hard to like others — it's because they don't really like themselves in the first place. That's why so many people's personal relationships with others cause them so much pain.

Maybe that lack of respect for yourself explains why some people appear almost desperate in their attempts to get others to like them. Parents often make complete fools of themselves trying to buy the affection and respect of their children. Let me tell you — you can't. Children, insecure in themselves, longing for love and affection from parents will even put up with verbal, physical, sexual and emotional abuse because they want to please and be loved. Boyfriends will spend money on demanding girlfriends — and vice versa — hoping to build a happy, loving relationship. A girl will say yes to sex when she would prefer to say no, except that she is too afraid to say so in case the boy stomps off and finds someone else who will say yes. You can't buy or manipulate a lasting relationship — short term perhaps but not long term and not a satisfying relationship, that's for sure.

Why do people resort to humiliating self-destructive tactics in order to be loved?

Because they don't like themselves and they believe they need someone else to like them — or pretend to — to give them that sense of acceptance, approval and esteem they're yearning for.

If you think about it, that kind of esteem is second-hand self-esteem. It's a fake, temporary and shaky confidence which, built on someone else's approval, collapses when they withdraw it.

It's also important to recognise that type of approval for what it is — another person's opinion. When I broadcast to maybe fifty thousand people, there are fifty thousand opinions of what I say. If I'm anxious for approval because I'm not confident about being me, which opinion will I take notice of? Can you see how impossible it is to build your self esteem on what other people think of you?

Sooner or later you have to arrive at that point of self-acceptance which allows you to stop trying to earn or deserve self-esteem. It dawns upon you like some exciting discovery — self-esteem is simply a case of self-acceptance. I can stop struggling.

Take Richard, a shy, self-conscious teenager who lacks confidence in himself and has a poor opinion of himself. The reason for his lack of self-respect is his belief that he is a loser — at a critical time in his life, when his friends are developing relationships with girls, he hasn't been able to attract someone special. He is constantly measuring his own personal worth or value by comparing himself with others, so he writes himself off as a failure because he hasn't got Miss Right. However, wonder of wonders, he strikes up a friendship with a girl. Richard is thrilled, feels more confident, and thinks his mates will respect him a little more — he's starting to feel he's not such an unlucky no-hoper after all. (That's how he had been feeling). Then the girlfriend loses interest, dumps Richard and he is shattered. Can you see the problem?

You can't base your opinion of yourself on someone else's approval or opinion of you.

You have to work out your own opinion so it's yours and no-one can take it from you. Otherwise, every time someone disapproves or withdraws their approval you are back to square one.

I believe one of the most important qualities for an enjoyable and satisfying life is having self-confidence and that means feeling at ease with yourself, feeling good about yourself — liking yourself.

Self confidence also gives you the courage to have a go. Self confidence tells you that you have the same rights as everyone else to set goals. Self-confidence tells you that you can reach for your goals and so achieve success.

Self-confidence gives you the freedom to make mistakes and cope with failure without feeling that your world has come to an end or that you are a worthless person.

Just in case you think this is a fairly recent discovery, let me assure you it is not. Seneca, the Roman statesman, author and philosopher who was born about 4 BC, said: 'Lack of self-confidence is not the result of difficulty; the difficulty comes from lack of confidence.'

Believe it or not, dear old Dr Norman Vincent Peale, the man who wrote the great book *The Power of Positive Thinking*, used to lack confidence. He once told me when visiting our studio for an interview that he was shy and self-conscious as a young man. Whenever he had to do something in front of people he used to wish a hole would open up for him to drop into. But he overcame it and went on to write, not just one book, but a heap of books on positive thinking and self-confidence in living. And he's been in demand all over the world as a public speaker. The man who was once awkward and negative about himself has become an inspiration and a teacher to millions. If he can do it, so can we.

I can remember teaching groups at the YMCA about positive mental attitudes. On the opening night some people were so shy they could hardly give their names and tell the group about themselves. Sometimes I saw that lack of self- confidence in the way they would walk, the way they talked or even the way they sat. It's called 'body language' and our body language says a lot about us. You know what I mean — the person who can't look you in the face, who hangs her head down. She's always looking at the floor. Sometimes I think she lost a dollar five years ago and she's still searching for it! What that self-conscious body language is revealing is that the person has poor self-image, little or no self-confidence. By the end of the eight week session, the members of the group were almost different people. They were able to walk into the room with heads up, talk with other participants and contribute to discussions. What had happened? Nothing miraculous — they simply came to realise that they were as good as the next person as far as being a human being is concerned. And that's the first lesson in developing self-confidence.

As a human being, you are as good, as worthy, as your neighbour. As a human being you get ten out of ten.

Because we often don't understand how feelings of inadequacy and poor self-confidence have developed in our minds, we often react by trying to cover them up — a sort of personality patch-up job. Some of us act aggressively, believing that aggression will convince others we know what we are doing. That reminds me of some sort of childish game of bluff. You can get away with it for a while. Trouble is, while you may be able to deceive others, you can't fool yourself.

Some people let themselves become overwhelmed by despair and give up trying to understand and attempting to do something about it. They hope that, in time, if they put up with it, they'll be able to forget their problem or that they'll wake up one morning, the problem will have miraculously disappeared and they'll feel confident, have overcome their shyness and a whole new world will open for them. Rather than try to analyse the problem and find the cause for the bad self-image, some just keep saying to themselves, 'I'm OK, I'm OK (I hope!)' Some people need a little 'chemical courage' so they turn to alcohol or drugs.

I don't think we solve problems that way. We may be able to distract ourselves for a while but, ultimately, the lack of confidence lets us down when we least expect it and when we really don't want it. Remember when you were in school and you didn't know the answer to a question? My trick was to appear busy, hoping the teacher would target someone who was gazing around the room. Sometimes it worked. Sometimes she picked on me and my ignorance would be exposed. Pretending or sticking the head in the sand never really solves anything. Sooner or later the pressure is applied and the truth comes out. It is better to develop self-confidence than to live in fear.

So where do we find the self-confidence or self-esteem we are looking for?

How do we develop a healthy, comfortable feeling about the person we are? More importantly, how do we maintain that feeling?

Self-confidence or self-esteem is the product of a good self image.

Self image put simply, is the idea or picture we carry in our minds of what we think we are really like. Ever carried a picture of someone you like in your wallet or purse? Our self image is like that, except it is the picture of ourselves we carry in our minds. Unfortunately, the self-image picture of the mind is not always as accurate as a photograph. Sometimes

23

like some photographs it is out of focus, blurred or just plain wrong. Often we are acutely aware of our self-image and for a while it is never far from our thoughts. At other times it is buried deep in the subconscious mind underneath a whole heap of long forgotten memories and experiences. Although buried, our self-image (the way we think about ourselves) actively influences our thoughts and attitudes far more than we realise. Psychologists have discovered that *how we see ourselves influences the way we respond to the experiences we encounter from day to day.*

The best way to explain this idea of self-image is to use an illustration. Think of your favourite colour. At the same time, think of the colour you dislike most. Next, imagine you have been invited to a party and the event is special enough to justify a new dress or jacket for the occasion. So you go shopping. You walk into the store and there on the rack is an outfit you really like, available in two colours — the colour you like and also the colour you dislike. Which do you choose? Naturally you choose your favourite colour. Why? Because you think it's the colour that makes you look your best. That mental process of deciding which to buy is fascinating isn't it? It's a bit like a video screen in the head. First, you imagine yourself in the favourite colour and you approve of what you see. Then you imagine yourself in the colour you dislike. Somewhere along the line in the decision process, you like what you see on the video screen in your mind and that then becomes your choice.

That video screen of the mind is interesting. It plays a huge part in our self-image. On it, we see ourselves and the image we see is an image that has built up over years. But it's not a silent movie. It has sound and our inner voice tells us that we look good in that colour, that we look bad in the other, disliked colour.

How is that self-image formed?

Our self-image is the product of a lifetime of experiences and attitudes. Once upon a time it was popular to blame everything on our childhood. But in recent times we've come to realise that people of seventeen, thirty or forty-five can encounter a shattering experience, such as a serious illness or an accident, a broken relationship or business failure which can dramatically affect their thinking about themselves and consequently their behaviour.

Our mind is very much like a video recorder, building up a memory bank of ideas and images about us from little scraps of information, comments, experiences and impressions gathered over a lifetime — whether that lifetime for you at the moment is fifteen, twenty or fifty years. Most of us don't bother to challenge that self-image picture because it has been building up quietly, unnoticed for so long.

25

All the experiences we have been through, the things people have said to us and about us, our achievements, failures, knocks and successes, have all been recorded on to the tape along with our interpretations and attitudes to those events. We come to accept the picture and to believe in it. But that picture may be wrong because the way we thought about these events or interpreted them has been wrong.

The funny thing about humans is that we seem more willing to believe the criticisms than the compliments or praise. That can be disastrous! If our self-image is crippled by negative, destructive ideas, then the mind can end up sending us self-destructive messages and we can become negative people, destroying ourselves through negativity and failing to realise our potential.

That's not to suggest we should ignore criticism, particularly when it is constructive and offered by a friend wanting to help us.

So how well do you know yourself? Socrates the Greek philosopher observed that **'the unexamined life is not worth living'**. I believe it is vital that we should understand ourselves and if we want to do that we have to understand how we developed the unique self-image we have built up in our minds and which now influences our actions.

A Canadian neurologist, Wilder Penfield did some

experimental work with the human brain, probing it to try to stimulate forgotten memories and experiences. In his notes on those experiments he wrote: 'The evidence seems to indicate, that everything which has been in our conscious awareness [in other words, those events and experiences we have had] is recorded and stored in the brain and is capable of being in the present.' Penfield found, when touching certain sections of the patient's brain with a probe, that the patient could recall previously forgotten experiences and even hear piano music long forgotten. In other words, the brain is like a huge natural computer with everything stored away but able, under certain circumstances, to recover that stored material and bring it to the surface to be enjoyed, to encourage or to threaten and frighten.

When I was twenty I once got severely sunburnt. That night, the family I was staying with for the weekend served the most delicious sponge dessert with chocolate chips through it. I thoroughly enjoyed the dessert but during the night I was violently ill, not from the dessert, but because of the sunburn. I was sick and sorry for myself for the whole weekend. It was agony. Even now, thirty years later, whenever I see those chocolate chips, memories of that awful weekend come back. They act as triggers for the computer memory system to flash those details on to the screen of my mind. If you think about it for a moment, you can probably think of some 'triggers' that bring back specific memories — perhaps a piece of music, a movie, a photo, a souvenir. The action of the 'trigger' is a bit like pressing the recall button on the computer file in your mind.

If you find it hard to believe that the mind is able to store experiences away on your brain computer tape for future replay, have a talk to doctors, nurses or anyone who works with old people. Often, oldies may seem a little muddle-headed about what's going on at the moment or what happened yesterday but they will sometimes revert to childhood, remembering with amazing accuracy and detail names and events from fifty years back. There's not much doubt about Penfield's theory that the mind stores it all away. We've also come to realise that, even though stored away, those memories can be very influential on our day to day thinking and living.

A plastic surgeon, Dr Maxwell Maltz, found that often after he had done a wonderful job reconstructing a person's face following a serious accident, even though the face looked as good or better than before the accident, the patient would find it hard to get back into the stream of life; the scars were still in the mind, even though they were no longer on the face. Maltz made a study of this peculiar behaviour and found a whole new understanding of the way the mind works. In his great book *Psychocybernetics*, he talks about the image that people carried in their minds, an image that wasn't true, that didn't really match the personality of the person. Nevertheless, they believed the image, however wrong it was.

Maxwell Maltz found that people's opinions of themselves were sometimes as out of touch with reality as the old, out of focus snap shot I mentioned a few pages back.

By the way, what we're talking about here is a negative, paralysing image trapped in the mind and crying out to be changed. It's a different thing altogether to a guilty conscience which has come about because we've done something we believe is wrong and it's bothering us. That can be dealt with by taking a deep breath, plucking up the courage to take steps to right the wrong or face up to the consequences.

However, it's my experience that many people develop guilty consciences and apologise for something they've done, when in fact they've done nothing wrong at all. Have you ever met that kind of person — always apologising, always saying sorry, even when they've done nothing wrong? They have poor ideas about themselves and so they go through life apologising for their presence — almost as if they are apologising for taking up a little space, breathing a little air. There is no need to tiptoe through life apologising — we each have our right to be here, to enjoy and experience life to the full. It is possible to shake off that negative image as we'll explain through the following pages.

'no one can make you feel inferior without your consent'

Brainwashing Starts Early

Think of some of the experiences that can have profoundly negative effects in our lives, incidents from childhood and our growing years, such as growing up poor, painfully aware of the things other kids had which you didn't, such as pocket money, a bike, holidays. Maybe you were teased because you had big ears, too much puppy fat or you were very tall or short. Children can be quite cruel in their ridicule. Perhaps your parents divorced and you blamed yourself for it. What about the impact on us of cruelty and abuse, physical or verbal? What about the put downs you may have experienced as a youngster because you were not a high academic achiever, because your spelling was poor or you never won a prize in athletics?

I was talking with a twelve year old boy one day and I sensed that there was something wrong. I said to him, 'I get the idea you don't feel too good about yourself.' 'I don't,' he said, 'I'm a no hoper.' That was the picture he was building up in his mind about himself. Who told him that? Was it his teacher, a parent, some of the kids at school? If that's what he is thinking at the age of twelve, what is he going to be thinking about himself by the time he's sixteen or twenty?

Psychologists talk about the looking glass or mirror effect to explain that how we see ourselves is often based on what we think other people are thinking or saying about us. So we reflect in our behaviour the person we think they judge us to be. Children who are told, directly or indirectly, that they are failures will come to label themselves as incompetent. It's called 'self-labelling' and once that self-labelling occurs, future failure is almost guaranteed because the child expects to fail. Because she expects to fail, she becomes half-hearted in her efforts, so she does fail and then says, 'See, I told you I couldn't do it.'

That expectation of failure doesn't just apply to children, it can also apply to wives or husbands who are constantly being put down by their partners, parents who are put down by children, children who are put down by parents and employees who are put down by the boss. Make a point of listening to the way people speak to one another. Make a note of the number of times people speak with a sting in the sentence, for example: 'Hurry up, stupid, and get into the car.' 'Come on, clumsy, and clean up your mess' and so on.

I'm not suggesting that all failure is due to a mental attitude that expects to fail, but a lot of it is.

We need to remind ourselves that. just because we try, we are not automatically guaranteed first place. And once we convince ourselves, we can show our children and our friends what winning means. Winning is sometimes a slow process of constantly improving on our past record. If we persevere and keep improving on our last effort we steadily move up the ladder of achievement.

An American psychiatrist, Fritz Perls, once wrote, 'Most of us were brought up in the atmosphere of disapproval.' When I first read that, I thought, 'Just a minute, I may not be the perfect father, but I'm sure that's not true.' But when you think about it, so much of our communication with our children is negative isn't it? We say things like, 'Who left the lights on — it looks like Disneyland. Who left the bath running — there's a tidal wave coming down the hall. Whose bike is that in the garage, under the car?'

Because we love our children we feel the need to constantly care for them and that can lead us to constantly correcting them, always supervising them and that can lead to the youngster feeling that his or her parents are always finding fault, always nagging, always negative. We also need to look for opportunities to encourage our children.

Sometimes, teachers, parents, husbands, wives, employers and even so-called friends can say some pretty cruel things: 'You're hopeless, you're stupid, you're a bad person.' We are often quick to hand out criticism which can be destructive and damaging. I'm not suggesting that we should never offer constructive, helpful criticism. However, we do tend to adopt the attitude that if someone is doing something correctly, then that doesn't need encouragement. But it does. Make sure the praise is sincere and genuine — there's nothing less encouraging or insulting to your intelligence than someone handing out insincere praise.

I remember an old teacher I had at school. It didn't matter how bad your essay was, he always found something to praise before going on to make constructive suggestions to improve it — spelling, grammar, sentence construction. He never overlooked mistakes but he didn't start on them — he began on a complimentary, encouraging note. It always made it easier to take the corrections. As Mary Poppins used to sing 'a spoonful of sugar makes the medicine go down.'

34

Some parents have gone to 'school' to learn how to be better parents at Parent Effectiveness programs. These are training sessions for parents eager to learn how to improve their performances as parents. PE programs stress the importance of commenting on the action rather than resorting to the all too common reaction of blaming and humiliating the person. That way the child can be corrected without suffering damage to his or her self-esteem. For example, why say 'You are a stupid, hopeless boy because you failed to do well at school this year'? Rather, look for some sign of improvement, encourage the child and then take steps together to plan what can be done to improve — some extra work from the teacher, something you can do together or maybe some remedial coaching. It's my observation that most children want to do well at school — just as most people want to do well in life — but many become convinced they can't, so they give up and pretend it doesn't matter to them.

Your childhood may have been a nightmare and as a result you've grown up with a terrible self-image. On the other hand, you may have grown up in a fairly normal sort of household but still have a poor self-image because you got little encouragement and your folks paid little attention to the need to build your self-esteem. Some parents are reluctant to encourage their children too much in case they become conceited or arrogant so they make the mistake of offering very little praise and encouragement, unaware that their child is growing up with a stunted, handicapped self-image. As a father of five children let me make this observation, I believe it's important to provide the atmosphere for children to tackle a variety of hobbies, sports, interests and to encourage them as they do so. I also believe it's important to realise that failure or making mistakes is not the end, but simply part of the learning process.

You may have lost confidence in yourself at seventeen because of a particular failure or disappointment. It is important to remember that this issue of self-image doesn't only apply to children and their parents, it also involves employers and employees, husband's attitudes to wives and children's attitudes to parents. You may have made it to twenty or thirty and then had a relationship go sour or a business venture collapse and the result is a giant scar on that self-image of yours — a scar which now influences your thinking every time you go to take a chance. The inner voice of the mind says to you, 'You can't do this, because the last time you tried, you failed. You're a failure.' Joe Alexander, a communications teacher, called that inner voice of negativity 'the inner saboteur'.

The remarkable thing about that negative inner voice, that inner saboteur, is that we listen to it so attentively. We give it an authority it doesn't deserve. As Eleanor Roosevelt, wife of a former President of America, said, '**No one can make you feel inferior without your consent.**'

Think about that quote for a little while. If someone tries to put you down, if someone tries to insult you or humiliate you, their words will only affect you if you accept the words and give authority to them. If you have a poor self-image it is likely you will accept the put down. If you think of yourself negatively and feel almost apologetic for taking up some space on the earth, then you will agree with the insult and allow it to damage your emotions and self-esteem. However, it will all depend on whether you permit someone to make you feel inferior. It all depends on your consent.

Five Ideas for Developing a Better Self-Image

1. Stop comparing yourself with others

Why? Because you don't have to. You are a unique, one-off model! No other person in the world is exactly like you. There never has been and there never will be. Some may be better looking, taller, more athletic, fitter, more intelligent, better singers, better cooks, better public speakers. But **no-one, absolutely no-one, can do a better job of being you!** Your parents may nag you, your wife may try to organise you, your husband may try to dominate you, your boss may try to do your thinking for you but no-one can climb inside your head to do your

39

thinking for you. Only you can send the signals to the muscles that put body, mouth and eyes into action. You are it.

I remember interviewing Professor Max Howell and his wife Dr Reet Howell. They had written a book about all the Olympic gold medal winners in Australia's history. As I talked with Max and Reet Howell I was fascinated by the idea of being one of those gold medal winners. Think about it — there you are, standing on the winner's stage receiving the gold medal. For that exciting moment you know that you are the best in the world in that event. The packed arena roars approval and praise. The speakers boom with your country's national anthem and you watch your nation's flag rising to the top of the mast. The world applauds you. You bow and the Olympic official places the ribbon over your head and you feel the weight of the gold medal on your chest. You are the best in the world.

Now you may not be much of an athlete but I want you to imagine yourself standing on the number one stage. Why are you there? Not because you are the record holder for some athletic event. You are on the number one stage because you are the only one of your kind in history! There never has been another you, there never will be. If your name is John or Mary Smith there may be plenty of people in the world with that same name. But you know **you are a one and only, unique human being**. So you can stop comparing yourself and feeling overshadowed by others and start doing something worthwhile with that special life that is your exclusive property and responsibility.

Doesn't that give you a fantastic sense of freedom? It is like chains dropping off your mind.

Shakespeare wrote: 'All the world's a stage and all the men and women merely players.' In your life, on your stage, you've not only got the leading role, you are also writing the script and directing the action!

A friend of mine, the Reverend Ted Noffs of the Wayside Chapel in Kings Cross, Sydney, developed a new positive approach to drug education and his Life Education Centres are spreading all over Australia. Instead of trying to terrify young people with horrific stories of what drugs can do to you, Ted and his small army of workers explain to small children and teenagers how wonderful their bodies are, how unique they are. Kids are taught 'I'm my own boss'. The education program is working and that's a lesson we've all got to learn — I am my own boss!

When I suggest you stop comparing yourself, I don't mean that we can't learn from others, or that we shouldn't model ourselves on other successful people. Of the people I've met who are having trouble with their self-image, most constantly compare themselves unfavourably with others.

That negative comparison paralyses them. They are frightened to make the attempt, because they believe they can't do it as well as someone else.

I'm told that Irving Berlin, who wrote the best-selling songs *White Christmas* and *God Bless America*, had only two years at school and no formal education in music at all. As a small boy he sold newspapers on street corners and earned a living for a while as a singing waiter in New York's Chinatown. You would think that would stop a budding song-writer in his tracks. But it didn't stop him writing some of the greatest songs and musicals of all times.

> **Don't let what you don't have stop you from using what you do have**.

Lots of people are better than I am at a variety of activities but I don't feel depressed because I'm not yet as good as they are. I learn from them because, if they can do it, someone else must also be able to do it. Why not me? Why not you? The words of the scientist Sir Isaac Newton are worth remembering: *'If I have seen further, it is by standing on the shoulders of giants.'*

It is worthwhile to analyse the style and performance of people we admire. They act as role models or mentors for us. I admire their ability and their success. But I don't envy them. Envy turns us sour, resentful and jealous. Admiration inspires us to adapt their successful strategies into our own game plan. By all means, observe the way successful people do it but don't make your life a carbon copy. The key is to adapt their winning techniques and build them into your own life. I've seen and heard many young radio announcers copy some of the nation's best broadcasters but they never achieve the success of their idols. Who wants a carbon copy when you can hear the original? Better to develop your own unique self, using the winner as an example only.

Let me make this observation about people with a good self-image and healthy self-esteem. Their healthy self-image doesn't depend on putting other people down. Often you meet people who, every time they open their mouths, are putting someone down, criticising and ridiculing. You can be sure they have a problem with their own self-image and they're trying to resolve that by struggling to the top of the heap by putting others underneath them. There is no need to. Because you are a unique one-off model you can win without destroying someone else in the process. That's what is commonly called the win/win or double win situation.

Our society tends to place so much emphasis on winning that we are tempted to win at all costs. The well-balanced person with the good self-image, the healthy self-esteem, can encourage the situation where the other person walks away without loss of face and without damaged self-esteem.

2. Stop trying to please everybody

When we try to please everybody, we are looking for their approval because we haven't yet come to the point where we approve of ourselves. It is impossible to please everybody.

> Self-esteem cannot come from other people.

If you depend on others for your feeling of self-worth, it isn't self-worth at all — it is a sense of worth or self-respect depending on other people's approval. Needing other people's approval of yourself is like saying 'your approval of me is more important than my own opinion of myself'. That's not to say it isn't perfectly natural to ask the opinion of someone you admire or respect.

The need for approval is very strong. Small children bring their latest work of art to parents for their approval. Half the time you can't be sure you're even holding it the right way up! They have to explain what the confusion of coloured lines are about. And we encourage them, don't we? We know they need praise and they'll be shattered and hurt if we ridicule their efforts. But it would be sad if the child failed to mature and at the age of twenty five was afraid to attempt anything without the approval of others. Yet many people go through life, 'living lives of quiet desperation' as Thoreau described it, because they are afraid to try in case they fail. Let me make this point in passing: it's a shame some parents get to a point in the growth of their child when they seem to think praise and encouragement are no longer important. It doesn't matter how old we are, a little recognition is always appreciated.

One fable told by Aesop is about an old man and his grandson taking a donkey to market to sell. They set off along the road to the village, leading the donkey and talking happily together. People they passed said, 'Look at those fools walking, when they could be riding that donkey.' So they rode the donkey until they heard people saying as they passed, 'Isn't that cruel, those two on that poor donkey.' So the lad walked happily alongside as the grandfather rode. But then people commented, 'How unfair for that old man to ride while the poor little boy has to walk.' So the boy rode and grandfather walked. You guessed it — then someone commented on how unfair it was for the boy to ride while the grandfather walked. Late that afternoon they struggled into town, grandfather in front, the little boy behind, with the poor old donkey strung on a pole, being carried.

Comedian Bill Cosby looks at it this way: **'The key to failure is trying to please everybody.'** The key word is everybody. Realising that we can't please everybody ought not make us hostile, unco-operative and difficult to live with, pleasing nobody. That approach to life would be just as disastrous as its opposite.

45

3. Stop blaming other people

We blame parents, teachers, society, the government, the media, poverty, our poor health — whatever we can find — to carry our excuses. You can just about get right through life blaming others and never taking responsibility for your own life. Sure your parents may have let you down, your teachers may have picked on you, you may have missed out on a lot because your family was poor. That's all yesterday stuff.

Blaming others is one of the biggest cop-outs of all time. It makes you feel so self-righteous as you wallow in your misery and depression. If that is all you want out of life, then carry on but if you want more out of life than that, then the time has come to sit up and take responsibility for your own life.

I went to visit a man in prison. He is a brilliant and talented man who had broken the law and was paying the price. As I sat talking to him in the grim prison surroundings he said, 'I must be the only guilty person here. Everybody else seems to be here because of a crooked policeman, an unsympathetic jury, a bad judge or a hopeless lawyer.' My opinion of him rose, simply because he wasn't trying to blame others but was facing up to his own guilt.

Carl Rogers, one of the great names in twentieth century psychology, says: 'We whine, nag, get irritable and become jealous simply because we are trying to blame others.' He says there is a way out of it — to own up to our own emotions and then decide to work on ourselves to change ourselves, rather than blaming others, complaining about others and hoping others will change.

4. Take responsibility for your own life

If you take responsibility for your own life and you start doing something significant with it, you won't have to say, 'It was nothing — my Mum or my wife or my boss did it for me.' You've got to take responsibility for your own life because, when it boils down to it, your life is run from inside your head — and you're the only one in there! It's wonderfully convenient trying to dodge the responsibility for running your own life. It can make you feel so self-righteous if you can find someone else to blame for all your misfortunes. You can play the game of getting others to make your decisions for you so that, if it doesn't work out, you can excuse yourself and blame someone else. It's so simple. But it's an enormous exercise in self-deception and passing the buck.

I want to stress the idea that we might as well do something significant with our lives because we only get the one shot. But significant is a word we have to define for ourselves. For some it's money, for others significant means being the top performer in a profession, career or trade. For someone else a great circle of friends and the enjoyment of all that life has to offer is more important. Whatever you do, don't waste life — don't fritter it away, day by day, week by week, like sand trickling through your fingers.

The Abbé Henri de Tourville wrote these encouraging words: 'Use all your intelligence and experience in managing your own life, employing the tenderness you would expect to find in a being of ideal kindness.'

5. Be logical with yourself

Psychologist Albert Ellis developed an approach to life called Rational Emotive Therapy. He illustrated the way we often react irrationally to a situation with an explanation based on an ABC of simple responses:

A is the action, the experience or incident that triggers your response or behaviour.

B is the belief or the attitude we hold about that action.

C is your behaviour or your response to the action.

Let's illustrate it this way. You get a phone call from Mary with whom you were planning to share a dinner date. You are told she now won't be going with you, because she has found someone else to go with. That's the A (activating) experience.

You are devastated by this news. How do you react? You could feel a wave of real anger. You may say to yourself, 'How dare she do this to me!' Or you could be plunged into a profound state of depression. You could say, 'Mary changed her mind because she doesn't like me any more. There must be something wrong with me. Nobody loves me. I'm just a no-hoper, a loner.' Depression sets in. Both the anger and the depression reactions, the C (responses) are negative. The inner saboteur has been at work undermining you. But just because Mary has chosen to go with someone else, there is no genuine reason to think the fault is yours.

Between **A** and **C** there is **B**, the beliefs we hold. Think about it — once we learn to control **B** (beliefs and attitudes) we can control **C** (responses). This is not an altogether new idea. In Shakespeare's play, Hamlet says, **'Things are not good or bad but our thinking makes them so'**.

Ellis says we need to dispute and challenge those irrational panic ideas and reactions which are based on our beliefs and attitudes. If we have a poor self-image, a poor idea about ourselves, then it's highly likely those reactions will heap all the blame on to ourselves. Have you ever done that?

Imagine this situation for a moment. Sure it is disappointing that Mary isn't going with you anymore but it is not the end of the world. Many of us react irrationally because we want everything our own way but life just doesn't work like that. That sort of irrational behaviour is a bit like some little child stamping her feet and putting on a tantrum in a store because her mother refuses to buy her what she wants. Sometimes we react irrationally because we panic or because our self-esteem is so low we immediately blame ourselves for the situation when in fact we are not to blame.

What are some of the other everyday situations that trigger irrational responses? Traffic jams are a classic example. Do you get angry and upset if the traffic doesn't flow smoothly and quickly? What's the point of getting emotional? Will it make a difference or simply make it more aggravating? Do you get annoyed when you are trying to phone home and the line is engaged? Do you blame your husband or children for gasbagging? Do you know why the phone is busy? Should the people at home realise that you are trying to call? Maybe you get angry because they're not telepathic. If you stop to think about it, there are dozens of examples of irrational responses to annoying situations. But the power to choose the response to that stressful situation is ours and ours alone.

Once you develop the routine of challenging irrational responses, it will amaze and excite you how much more quickly you can recover from disappointments and get on with living your life. It is vital to keep reminding yourself that in facing a situation when irrational panic seems about to engulf you, you do have a choice about your response.

How do you make that choice to challenge your responses? The simplest thing to do is to count to ten, take a few deep breaths to calm ourselves and then pause to ask a few searching questions. For example, 'Why am I responding in this way?' 'Am I drawing conclusions that are not logical and realistic?' 'Why am I imagining the worst result?' 'Why am I tipping the blame for this situation on myself?' 'What sensible solution can I see for this predicament?'

If you find it hard to be rational and logical to begin with, share your problem with someone you trust who can look at the situation more calmly and more objectively. That person may then be able to help you, step by step, to analyse your response and work out a more practical and realistic position.

No one said life is fair. It would be great if it was but it isn't. How many times have you heard someone say life isn't fair? Life is neither fair nor unfair. It just is. We need to develop techniques for coping with the knocks and the setbacks. One of the best ways I know is to start being honest with myself, stop blaming and start taking charge, taking responsibility for my own life. The other helpful quality I've found necessary to encourage in myself is the ability to laugh at myself occasionally and not to take myself too seriously. Make sense?

Dr Ellis's ABC theory on coping with life is a great help for people who wallow in self pity, dropping hints for family and friends to be sympathetic and supportive. It is usually an attention-seeking device exercised with remarkable manipulative skill by those who do it frequently. If you know you do it, make a resolution to try being more logical, more honest and more rational when you next run into this type of situation.

COMMITMENT

1. I will stop comparing myself with others.
2. I will stop trying to please everybody.
3. I will stop blaming other people.
4. I will take responsibility for my own life.
5. I will be logical and rational with myself.

Signature:_____

You may find it useful to copy these five lines down on a small card, carry it in your pocket and refer to it a couple of times a day.

Mistakes are Things You Do

Because of that rational attitude to life you are developing, it's important to realise that making a mistake is something you do, not something you become. You can have a failure, but you don't become one as a result. You can have a string of failures, for that matter, but you don't become a failure. Yet how often do you hear someone saying, 'I'm a failure. I'm hopeless. I'm stupid' or 'I told you it wouldn't work. I told you I couldn't do it.' That's the self fulfilling prophecy. That's the self-labelling at work and the negative self-talk of sabotage thinking.

There is no more certain way to fail than to keep telling yourself you will.

I remember interviewing Dr Roger Bannister. During the interview he mentioned that once he had broken the four minute mile, others found they were also able to do it. Once the mythical barrier had been broken down, others believed they could — and did. Another world famous athlete, Herb Elliot, the man regarded by many as the world's greatest mile runner, told me during an interview that the challenge for the athletic coaches and the athletes of the future is no longer the physical limit but breaking through the psychological limits — the limits of the mind. The writer Aldous Huxley puts it this way: **'Experience is not what happens to a man. It is what man does with what happens to him.'**

If you really are serious about developing a healthy self-image, and are starting to feel good about yourself, be prepared to grow. And you know the exciting part? You are never too old. I've met old people of twenty-five and young people of eighty. I remember leading a tour of China with listeners from my radio station. One of our group was eighty-two. She laughed all the way around China and she came away the following year on a trip through Europe. She thoroughly enjoyed herself and she was popular, making friends easily. Others much younger than her spoilt the trip for themselves and others because of their constant grumbling. So you are never too old to enjoy life, never too old to change.

After all, although your body stops growing, it is constantly changing. Skin is dying and being replaced daily. Cells are changing, even bones are changing. You are not the person today that you were yesterday. Your mind is also capable of changing, so why not develop and expand your mind as well?

'Few of us make the most of our minds. The body ceases to grow in a few years; but **the mind, if we will let it, may grow almost as long as life lasts.**' So said Sir John Lubbock in *The Pleasures of Life*.

A friend of mine is an activities organiser in a retirement village. Before she went there, lots of the oldies used to just sit and watch the world go by as age crept on. Lorraine is an energetic bombshell of a lady and she has them doing physical exercises, running their own concerts, quiz contests, outings, trips and other activities which would wear out the average forty year old. She asked me to compere a concert one night at the Village: oldies in their late seventies and eighties were doing physical exercise routines that I couldn't do and they had a general knowledge when it came to quiz questions that would leave you standing open-mouthed. Lorraine has seen old folk coming to the retirement village to die and in six months they've been running around as if they've discovered the secret of eternal youth.

Her motto is: 'Use it, before you lose it'. You are never too old to change, even though changing is not always easy.

Ask yourself: 'Am I frightened of change?'

A lot of people are because they feel threatened by change — and that's understandable. They reckon the only person really interested in a change is a wet baby. We feel threatened because we feel insecure. Murray Banks used to say, 'The only permanently adjusted people are in cemeteries.'

Good self-esteem frees us to be more creative and adventurous, to welcome change. It allows us to open our minds because we are not threatened or frightened by new ideas. We form friendships more easily because we are at ease and comfortable with ourselves and, as a result, open-minded, and not threatened by others. We become participators, not spectators paralysed by the fear of failure or other people's comments. We become winners.

Self-confidence, which flows from a good self-image, is a bit like riding a bike — success breeds success.

Can you remember when you first learned to ride a bike? That afternoon is vivid in my memory. My brother Clem steadied the bike while I got on and he held the back of the seat and ran behind me down the hill. It was a glorious sense of achievement and freedom. I felt as if I was flying. I was so thrilled by the sensation, I called to my brother to tell him how good it felt. He wasn't there. He'd let go! I'd been riding the bike by myself. But I couldn't ride on my own, not yet. This was my first day. So I did what every self-respecting beginner would do — I fell off. My brother looked down at me, lying on the ground groaning. He reminded me that I could ride on my own — I had just done it.

Talking about bike riding, years later I can relate to that great twentieth century philosopher Linus, friend of Charlie Brown and Snoopy, who once said, 'Life is like a ten speed bike — most of us have gears we never use.' The successful people in life are those who persevere, who never quit, who form the habit of doing the things other people give up on. If you aim to achieve some success every day, no matter how small or humble that success may seem — read a chapter of the book you've been planning to start, cut down your smoking, say no to that extra cream bun, walk the stairs instead of taking the lift — even small successes will give you that buzz of achievement which encourages you to keep going.

Take a look at your posture — the way you stand, the way you sit. People reveal their lack of confidence through their body language. Start walking confidently, even if you have to start by practising it in the privacy of your room, in front of a mirror.

If you are fed up with feeling like a loser, if you are tired of thinking of yourself as second rate, if you've had enough of disliking yourself, remember this, no one needs to live one minute longer as he is — because we have been endowed with the ability to change. Desperation is as good a motive for change as any other I can think of. Deep down you want to change but the job might look formidable and too big for you. Try, then, to remember this quote from the Reverend Robert Schuller: 'By the mile it's a trial; by the yard it may be hard but inch by inch — it's a cinch.'

Attitudes
Are Important

One of the ideas that has most influenced my thinking is this one from psychologist William James: '**The greatest discovery of my generation is, that a person can alter his life, by altering his attitude of mind.**'

Just think about that for a while. It is one of the most significant, one of the most exciting truths of all time. How often have you wanted to alter your life because you are depressed, because you are in a rut or because you've done something that is bugging you? Do you feel as if you're trapped in a revolving door and can't get out? You feel powerless, helpless

— not knowing how to change. The answer lies within your own mind and its remarkable powers. Victor Frankl, a man who spent years of his life in a German concentration camps, wrote, '*Man's greatest freedom is his ability to decide the attitude he will take to something.*'

If past experiences, and things said to us in the past influence the self-image we have of ourselves today and if we allow past images, thrown up on the screens of our minds, to lead us to act in a certain way, then we can also use images or pictures of the future to influence our behaviour. If what is in our past can influence us, so can those things before us — in our futures.

You don't win races looking over your shoulder, you win them by concentrating on the finishing line in front. You don't win in sport just kicking or throwing the ball around aimlessly, you win by aiming for the goal posts. What motivates you to save money? Wanting something. Wanting something you haven't got influences you to save, to sacrifice and go without, so you can have it.

Your attitude to the future (wanting to buy a car, for example) influences the way you behave today (saving rather than spending money). Wanting to lose weight influences the way we eat. Wanting to impress the girlfriend, boyfriend or business associate influences our behaviour. What we want in the future influences our behaviour, choices and plans today.

Karl Menninger, psychiatrist and founder of the Menninger Institute, said: '**Attitudes are more important than facts.**'

If you find that hard to believe, let me illustrate it. Scientists at La Trobe University's Brain Behaviour Research Institute, aggravate rats to simulate the sort of stress experienced by the average executive. (I've heard of the rat race. Could this be how they invented the term?) The rats are given electric shocks at the sound of a buzzer. Once they learn to associate the buzzer with the shock, the scientists eliminate the shock but, at unexpected intervals, sounds the buzzer. Even though the rat is no longer getting the shock, the sound of the buzzer still causes the rat distress. The rat has learned to respond. The rat is no longer getting the shock, but behaves as if he is. In other words, his attitude is more influential than the facts. You may be interested to know that when they dissect the rats they find advanced arterial disease. Rats of the same age and breeding, fed on the same diet without the buzzer and shock routine, have healthy arteries. That gives you some idea of the impact of stress in our lives.

Greg Carey, a broadcasting colleague of mine, told me the story that some horse trainers used a battery device during the training of their race horses. As you will appreciate, the use of the prod is strictly illegal in a race. However, if the jockey screams into the horse's ear during training gallops and uses the prod it shocks the poor old horse into a dramatic

61

increase in speed! On the day of the race, without the prod, the jockey can simulate the training experience of the horse by screaming into his ear. The horse increases speed probably anticipating that the prod is going to give him a shock at any moment.

What do we mean when we talk about attitude? Attitude is simply the way we choose to see things and I stress that word *choose*. We do make a choice about the way we react, the way we view things and events. William Blake, the poet, once wrote these words: 'A tree is something so incredibly beautiful that it brings tears to the eyes. To others, it is just a green thing that stands in the way.'

I remember being in beautiful Penang in Malaysia with my daughter Jennifer. It was only a year or two after I'd been in hospital battling with cancer for my life. I'd been watching the paragliding for a while and I was hooked. Now I'm no Indiana Jones, so I didn't think I was taking too big a risk. After all, other people were doing it and the same number that went were coming back and they were all coming back alive.

Paragliding would have to be one of life's great experiences. They lay out a parachute on the beach behind you, harness you into it and then connect the harness via a long rope to a motor boat. I can tell you, it's a fascinating experience watching that long coil of rope snaking out as the motor boat takes off out to sea. You can't help wondering what's going to happen when the rope runs out — am I going to go shooting off down the beach after the boat, dragging the parachute? I'm here to tell you that when the rope does go taut, you only have to take a few running steps and the 'chute fills with air and you are lifted off the sand to follow the boat, but suspended in the air, held aloft by the parachute and pulled along down below by the speed boat. Well, I'm busily putting on my parachute harness and Jen comes running breathlessly up the beach.

'What on earth do you think you're doing?' she demands.
'Going paragliding,' I say, trying to appear cool and nonchalant.
'But you're forty-seven!' she gasps.
'Yes,' say I, 'and if you don't let me go, I'll be forty-eight!'

My loving daughter was terrified for my safety. My attitude was different. I'd been watching for about an hour and it looked quite safe to me. I was right. It was safe and it was a fabulous, memorable experience. Ten minutes later, Jenny was off to get her purse to pay for the same experience. What makes it exciting to one person and threatening to another? Attitude.

Some years later, I had the chance to go up in a hot air balloon. That was another wonderful experience. We gently lifted off the ground as the balloon filled with hot air and drifted over the city, across

some of the suburbs of beautiful Brisbane and
landed on the grass at the airport. The view was
spectacular. The experience of gliding across the
city was sensational and I was really excited as I
described it to some friends. Their reactions were
interesting. Some were excited. One was so threatened by the mere thought of going up above chair
height that the palms of his hands started to
perspire. Another friend, who has done a lot of
flying, said he wouldn't go unless the cane basket
came up to his chin. And another person's comment
really staggered me. He said, 'Who'd want to go in
a hot air balloon. All you'd see would be a lot of
rusty old roofs!' What's the difference in the reactions? Attitude.

And that's all that positive thinking is — you taking
control of your attitudes, taking control of your
mind and deciding to act in a positive, rather than a
negative way. I guess we've all met the cynics who
ridicule the whole idea of positive thinking. Some
people think it's irrational. Others think it's
ignoring the obvious and the inevitable and hoping
it will all go away by morning. That's not positive
thinking. That's stupidity!

Positive thinking is not sitting with fingers crossed,
hoping for the best. Positive thinking is not mumbo
jumbo; it's just another term for the constructive
attitude we choose to adopt when making a
decision, trying to cope, solving a problem or
dealing with a crisis. We can look at it negatively

with an attitude of gloom, despair and defeat or we can face up to it, calling on all our resources of optimism, courage and determination. A Roman philosopher, Epictetus, who lived in the first century AD said, **'People are not disturbed by events, but by their view of events.'** — in other words, their attitudes.

> *It's not so much a question of what happens to us — it's how we respond to it and what we do about it.*

How do we choose the best attitude?

It's not as hard as we may think.

I believe the decision process for attitude is no different from choosing between two cakes on a plate. What makes it hard is choosing to be positive if in the past we have frequently chosen to be negative. That takes determination on our part and the repeated decision to respond positively. It is important to remember that it is a matter of choosing to adopt either a positive or a negative attitude but it is a choice nevertheless.

If the experiences of the past can build up an image in our minds and influence the way we behave, so can the pictures from the future. Picturing what we want to be or want to achieve or want to possess, if it is done repeatedly, can superimpose new images and goals on our minds and our subconscious mind starts to respond to that forward-looking, positive attitude as opposed to a backward-looking, negative attitude.

I know that may sound hard to believe but it does work. It may be slow at first because you have become accustomed to thinking and reacting negatively. Persevere. Don't give up. Be prepared to visualise the new you, the new job, the new goals every day. When you do it, believe you can, believe you will achieve those goals but don't only believe — back your belief with hard, determined effort and be wholehearted in your positive belief.

You may feel positive thinking won't work every time — particularly when it's a new experience and you are trying to train your mind to choose a positive rather than a negative approach. However, it's still a better way of coping with problems, than negative thinking which will sabotage your life.

'the chief function of the body is to carry your brain around'

Your Most
Valuable Asset

I don't know why we pay so little attention to our minds — maybe it's because we got them for nothing. Most of us look after our dogs better than we care for our minds. How much money or time have you spent on your mind recently? How much effort have you spent to improve it, to expand it, to exercise it, to enrich it? Compare that with the time and money that have gone into clothes, records, entertainment, cosmetics, hair, luxuries and junk. Thomas Edison reckoned that **'The chief function of the body is to carry your brain around'**. Many of us spend more on the carriage than we do on the valuable cargo.

Every second magazine you pick up these days reminds you of the importance of at least some physical exercise. We also need to exercise our minds. We need to feed them with good, stimulating, thought-provoking books, lectures, tapes and films. And just as the body can't survive on a diet of junk food, neither can the mind. We need to spend a few dollars on our most valuable asset. We need not only to feed our minds but to exercise them as well, stretching them with brain teasers and new ideas that will tear down some of the old, self-imposed limits. Oliver Wendell Holmes, an early American writer, said: **'Man's mind, stretched to a new idea, never goes back to its original dimensions.'**

Dr Edward de Bono, who made Lateral Thinking a common phrase, believes that thinking can be taught. Educators are starting to agree with him and 'thinking' is now being taught in schools all over the world. How many lessons did you get on 'thinking' in school?

If you are wondering how to exercise your mind, try this idea from psychologist William James: 'Keep alive in yourself the faculty of making efforts by means of little useless exercises every day; that is to say, be systematically heroic every day in little unnecessary things; do something every day for the sole and simple reason that it is difficult and you would prefer not to do it, so that when the cruel hour of danger strikes, you will not be unnerved or unprepared. A self discipline of this kind is similar

Your Most Valuable Asset

to the insurance that one pays on one's house and possessions. To pay the premium is not pleasant and possibly may never serve us, but should it happen that our house were burnt, the payment would save us from ruin.'

If you want to improve on William James's idea, instead of doing 'little useless exercises' as he puts it, why not do something you've been delaying, something you don't want to do? That way, you get the benefit of the 'gymnastics of the will' exercise without doing something useless. Write the letter you've been meaning to write but have kept excusing yourself because you said 'I don't have the time.' What you really mean is 'I'm too lazy or too disorganised to make the time.' Phone someone you haven't spoken to for a while and say good day, even if you only chat for a few minutes.

Why are we too lazy?

Why don't we have the time?

I suggest the real reason is that, while we think something is important, it's not important enough to motivate us. We seldom put off doing what we really want to do.

Draw up a list of the ten things you don't want to do but have decided you must do. Put the toughest, most undesirable job on the top of the list. Then do it. The next day, do the second item on the list and

71

so on. No cheating and no starting at the other end. There is an enormous sense of achievement in doing this exercise.

> The simple fact of the matter is, **how we think, influences how we handle life**.

The Bible: says, 'As a man thinks, so is he.' The ancient Sanskrit writings of India, include this quote: 'Man is made by his beliefs. As he believes, so is he.' Buddha said, 'All that we are is the result of what we have thought.' Paavo Nurmi, the great Finnish athlete who won six Olympic gold medals, put it this way: 'All that I am, I am because of my mind. My mind is everything. My muscles are just pieces of rubber.'

Ask the karate expert how he breaks the piece of timber or the stack of bricks. Some of the secret is in his strength and training but he will tell you that a significant part of his skill starts in his mind. In recent years we've come to realise that people can actually control their moods and even their high blood pressure by learning the simple techniques of bio-feedback. In our society we place enormous importance on our physical condition and we place a lot of emphasis on achievement through building a bank balance. I believe we'll also achieve more and get a lot more satisfaction and achievement out of life if we spend time developing our minds. *Our minds are our most precious possessions.*

Our bodies may not look as attractive at fifty as they did at twenty but our minds can improve and, with some attention, go on improving. And don't say you are too old. You're never too old! I know a wonderful lady by the name of Dr Elsie Harwood. Dr Harwood and a colleague of hers, the late Dr George Naylor, gathered some retired people together to see if they could learn musical instruments and foreign languages. Eighty volunteers came to the University of Queensland to learn German. Their ages ranged from sixty-three to ninety-one.They took to the experiment like ducks to water. After only eight months, fifty-five of them were able to sit an exam translating German to English. Another eighty volunteers between the ages of sixty-five and eighty-nine joined a music class learning to play the recorder. The experiment spanned a period of some twenty one years and has been written up in professional journals as a resounding testimony to the ability of 'oldies' to continue learning. Don't let anyone tell you that you are too old to learn. Dr Harwood and Dr Naylor proved the lie of the old quote 'you can't teach an old dog new tricks'. Don't you believe it!

Dr Alex Comfort, in his great book *A Good Age*, talks about 'oldies' who started late in life. Fred Streeter, one of Britain's most famous gardeners, started broadcasting at the age of fifty-eight. He broadcast for forty years, till he was ninety-eight! Arthur Rubenstein gave one of the most remarkable performances of his life at the age of eighty-nine at

Carnegie Hall. Duncan MacLean won a silver medal at the 1975 Veterans' Olympics in Canada when he ran two hundred metres in forty-four seconds. He was ninety years old. Marian Hart flew solo across the Atlantic in a single-engined Beechcraft in 1975 at the age of eighty-four. She didn't learn to fly until she was fifty-four. Florrie Ball was riding her motorcycle in Lancashire, England at the age of seventy-seven. So you're never too old, are you?

Where do the great inventions come from? The mind. Where do the great works of art, the exciting pieces of music, the magnificent volumes of literature come from? The mind. Whether it is constructive or destructive, worthwhile or degrading, positive or negative — it comes from the mind. Cardinal Newman in one of his Oxford University sermons commented: 'Almighty God influences us and works in us, through our minds, not without them or in spite of them.'

If you haven't thought much about your mind and the role it plays in your life, this could all sound a bit theoretical — but it isn't. If your car is playing up you check the motor. If things aren't running smoothly in your life, check your motor — your mind. For some strange reason many of us forget that the mind works on at least two levels — conscious and subconscious. The conscious can actually 'program' the subconscious. If you don't program it, you could be leaving it to be programmed by other influences in your life. Remember the quote 'as a man thinks, so is he'.

Sometimes I think of the mind as a sponge that just goes on soaking up every little bit of information, every experience, comment and attitude. Like a sponge, it absorbs good things and bad things, constructive and destructive information. Occasionally I think you have to squeeze out some of the negative, destructive information about yourself. That doesn't mean we ignore our weaknesses or less attractive qualities. We need to do something about them. But we also need to squeeze out a lot of the false and negative ideas about ourselves.

The great American statesman Benjamin Franklin was once told by a good friend that he had become so critical, cynical and resentful that his friends were fed up with him. Franklin took that constructive comment from his friend and examined himself, listing those qualities he wanted to get rid of and set to work getting them out of his life. Benjamin Franklin became an outstanding leader, diplomat and father figure to the young nation of America. He left his mark on the history of that great country and the world. I wonder what would have happened if he had ignored the advice and and stumbled blindly on.

Many of us find it hard to grasp this idea of the conscious mind being able to program the subconscious. Think of any job that was demanding at first and then became easier as we mastered it. Learning to type, driving a car, operating a computer are all simple, common examples. At first you had to concentrate and almost send messages to hands and muscles.

When I was learning to drive a car I thought I needed a couple of extra feet and arms. Remember the first lesson? If it wasn't an automatic there was that awful business of letting the clutch out gently while you pressed down on the accelerator. If you didn't get the process right, the car used to kangaroo hop up the street. And usually the neighbours would all be out watering their gardens and giving those patronising smiles learners hate. I began to wonder if it would ever be as easy for me as for my driving instructor. I'm not sure of the precise moment at which it happened but, somewhere along the way (and it didn't take too long), the process that had at first required intense concentration became a simple non-threatening routine run from the subconscious control panel of my mind. So the conscious had programmed the subconscious. It happens all the time.

You can not only program your mind to drive a car, use a typewriter, a sewing machine or coordinate arms and legs to play tennis — you can also program it to stop slipping into negative, defeated attitudes every time you are confronted with a problem.

If you want to alter your life in any way, start taking control of your mind.

If you are wondering how to do that, simply start by talking to your mind and giving your mind orders. If you are nervous because you've heard they put people away for that, don't panic. We all talk to ourselves some of the time but to avoid misunderstandings, don't do your self-talking aloud on a crowded bus or in the intense quiet of an orchestral concert!

Positive thinking is simply the intelligent, constructive exercise of your greatest asset, your mind and, like a parachute — it only works when it is open.

'most problems are really the absence of ideas'

Making It Work

How do you make positive thinking work?

Decide to make your life an adventure — a game. You will be confronted with problems and challenges. The negative thinker is overwhelmed by the awesome threat of it. The adventurer is excited by the challenge of it.

When confronted by a problem, don't panic in thinking about the obstacles and giving up.

Make a conscious effort to list, either mentally or on paper, the positive and constructive things you can do to resolve it. Gather whatever information you need to make the decision or take the necessary action. That may require research, reading or consulting people whose advice you trust. Concentrate on what you can do, not on what you can't.

Don't waste time and energy worrying about what you can't do, or what might happen. *Worry is rehearsing for failure.*

When you start practising this positive mental attitude, you may find it hard to begin with. You may be shocked to find that your first reaction to a tough or threatening situation is negative. That's understandable. It seems easier to think negatively in response to a situation because that way you don't have to struggle and you don't have to work at solving it. It's easy to slip into the rut of the negative response.

AA Milne, the man who wrote the delightful Winnie the Poo stories wrote, 'The third rate mind is only happy when it is thinking with the majority. The second rate mind is only happy when it is thinking with the minority. The first rate mind is only happy when it is thinking.' Henry Ford's comment is also worth remembering: **'Thinking is the hardest work of all — and that's why so few of us do it.'**

You may also find positive thinking tough going

because you are surrounded by so much which is negative. You've only got to read the first five pages of the daily paper or watch the first ten minutes of the news on television, to feel that it's a pretty gloomy old world out there.

You may feel overwhelmed by the odds when you are confronted by a problem or a crisis. Someone illustrated it well this way: the diamond miners patiently shift tons of earth for the sake of finding a few gems no bigger than your little thumb nail. It would be easy to become discouraged by the mountain of soil and overlook the value of the precious stones. It is easy to be overwhelmed by the size of the problem and overlook the value or the importance of the solution. Once you develop the positive thinking habit — and it is a habit — you'll be amazed how much more optimistic you become, how much sooner you are able to find solutions to problems.

Yet, for some strange reason, we often respond negatively to situations. Montaigne, the French philosopher, once wrote, 'Most of my life has been full of terrible disasters — most of which never happened.' Isn't that true for all of us? How many times have you lost sleep, or been unable to eat simply because your imagination ran riot with all the negative possibilities facing you and then things turned out OK? Three days later you ask yourself what on earth you were worrying about.

I guess the underlying cause is anxiety or lack of security. If we are confident, facing problems rationally and realistically, then that negative response has less of a grip on us. Remember when you were little and you were scared of the dark? Your parents reassured you and your own experience as you grew up taught you that after the dark came the morning and there was nothing to fear. Remember the first time you made a speech and had convinced yourself the floor would probably open and swallow you or the audience would hate you — and you survived? Maybe they even liked what you said and you asked yourself 'What was I worrying about?'

I remember spending a weekend relaxing with my wife and family at the Coast. One of my daughters brought along a huge jigsaw puzzle. It provided a lot of fun but there was one problem. We were under the impression that a couple of pieces were missing. So, if a piece was hard to find, the natural reaction was to think this must be one of those missing pieces. In many ways, that thought robbed the puzzle of its fun because we believed it would never be completed. That thought was on everyone's mind as we got the last couple of pieces in place and found that there were no pieces missing after all! We had played the whole game with that negative belief overshadowing our play. Isn't that also true of life?

Many of us live overshadowed by some negative

possibility or some nagging self-doubt. We are crippled before we begin. How about you?

We often confuse negative attitudes with depression. I think it's fairly normal to have highs and lows in physical and emotional life. A few late nights and a day full of stress can certainly sap your energy and bounce. If you do feel depressed over a period of time it is important to ask yourself why, seek to find the cause of that feeling and take positive steps to remedy it. However, it is worthwhile mentioning that some depression can have a physical cause. Not all depression is caused by worry; sometimes it is a medical problem in the functioning of the brain.

If you can't find a reason for your worry, go and see a doctor, a psychologist or an experienced counsellor. If your doctor is too busy to listen and simply prescribes tranquillizers or sleeping tablets, go and get a second opinion from another doctor or, better still, see a psychologist or counsellor who will spend the time listening to you. Short term use of a sedative or tranquillizer can be helpful but most doctors advise against long term use.

One of the products of a negative attitude is fear — and fear paralyses. The fear of failure prevents many people from even starting. We are afraid of other people's opinions, afraid of what others think about us, afraid of what they will say about us. We are frightened to start on a project, apply for a job, even afraid to join a conversation because we think negatively and feel defeated, even before we start. Shakespeare said: 'Our doubts are traitors and make us lose the good we often might win, by fearing to attempt.' Sydney Smith, an English clergyman, essayist and wit, wrote back in the 1700s: 'Every day sends to their graves obscure men whom timidity prevented from making a first effort.'

Let's face it, failure is a fact of life, as is grief, disappointments and making mistakes. However, I think we learn more from our failures than from our successes. We usually don't analyse our successes; we may enjoy them, celebrate them, even bask in the moment of glory they bring, but it's usually the setbacks, failures and frustrating disappointments that stop us in our tracks and make us ask why. Success is sweet, but failure can be the teacher if we develop the right attitude to it.

Sometimes we are reluctant to try because we fear failure and we fear what others might say. Abraham Lincoln had a courageous attitude: 'I do the very best I can, I mean to keep going. If the end brings me out alright, then what is said against me won't matter. If I am wrong, ten angels swearing I was right won't make a difference.'

Abraham Lincoln's story is worth repeating because it is so inspiring. His mother died when he was just nine years of age. He had no more than a year's formal education. He failed in his first attempt to be elected to the General Assembly of Illinois in 1832. He failed in business in 1835 at the age of twenty-six. It took him several years to pay off his debts but in the process he earned the nickname 'Honest Abe'. His sweetheart died. He decided to study law and used to ride and sometimes walk the 20 miles from Salem to Springfield to borrow books. He sought public office but was defeated at the age of thirty-two. He had a nervous breakdown.

Lincoln tried to enter Congress at thirty-four and lost the election and lost again at the age of thirty-five. He was elected to Congress in 1847 but failed to be re-elected in 1849, returning to Springfield believing that his political career was over. He sought election to the Senate in 1854 but failed, failing again in 1858 at the age of forty-nine. Three of his four sons died while quite young. Finally, in 1860 at the age of fifty-one, he was elected sixteenth President of the United States and served two terms as President before his assassination in 1865. In that time he made such a profound impact upon the people and the history of that great nation that his name is still heard on people's lips today. If that's not a positive attitude, I don't know what is.

Napoleon Bonaparte made a couple of interesting observations: 'The human race is governed by its imagination' and 'Impossible is a word from the dictionary of fools.' It's very easy to read quotes like that and let them pass without giving them much serious thought. If you do think about it though, you realise that the pioneers, the innovators, the risk takers are all people who imagined or dreamed that something could be done. Instead of being overwhelmed by the arguments explaining why it couldn't be, they found out how it could be done and did it.

A story is told about twin brothers. One was an optimist. One was a confirmed pessimist. Their parents were concerned and talked the problem over with a friend. She suggested that they try toning down the optimist in case he found life too much of a rude shock when he got out into the world. For the pessimist the friend recommended they should do everything in their power to encourage him and build up his confidence. So that Christmas they spent a fortune on the most expensive and exciting electric train for the pessimist. But when he saw it on Christmas morning he said sadly, 'Probably doesn't work anyway.' They did a terrible thing to the little optimist. In an attempt to bring him down to earth and teach him that life is not all it seems, they simply filled a small box with horse manure. The optimist took one look and let out a shout of joy, 'Oh boy, there's got to be a pony nearby.'

David the Psalmist wrote, 'My cup runneth over.' The optimist said, 'What a blessing.' The pessimist said, 'What a mess.'

The optimist looks out the window and sees a beautiful sunrise. The pessimist looks out but only sees the dirty spots on the window. Two men looked out through prison bars — one saw mud and one saw stars. How we see life and how we cope with life depends on attitude. Someone summed up this whole question of facing life with either a negative or a positive attitude this way:

If you think you are beaten, you are.
If you think you dare not, you won't.
If you like to win, but think you can't,
It's almost certain you won't.

If you think you'll lose, you're lost.
For out in the world we find,
Success begins with a person's will —
It's all in the state of mind.

If you think you're outclassed, you are.
You've got to think high to rise.
You've got to be sure of yourself before
You can ever win a prize.

Life's battles don't always go
To the stronger or faster man.
But sooner or later the person who wins
Is the one who thinks he can.

When we are confronted by a problem, a choice, a crisis, we can respond negatively or positively. The choice is entirely up to you. Responding positively doesn't make a problem go away, it simply enables you to handle that problem from a position of strength not weakness. It gives you the advantage, the positive edge.

Don't be frightened of opposition — after all a kite only rises against the wind, not with it.

A Roman poet, Horace, wrote these words: 'Adversity has the effect of eliciting talents which in prosperous circumstances would have lain dormant.'

Many years ago, I was walking past a shop in Singapore and saw a poster which only cost me two dollars. It was the best investment I've ever made. The poster simply says: '**Most problems are really the absence of ideas.**' I live my life by that philosophy.

Talking about solving problems, I once had a segment on my radio program in which I asked callers to share some amusing incident in which the man of the house tried his hand at cooking. Well, one lady had gone away for the weekend. Tea and toast were about her husband's limit when it came to cooking skills but he loved caramel sauce.

When she got home, she could smell caramel sauce from the front door! I understand that you can make caramel sauce by boiling condensed milk in a saucepan. Her husband knew about that much too. So he boiled the can of condensed milk in the saucepan but he was distracted by the football on

TV. The can boiled and boiled and boiled. You guessed it — the saucepan boiled dry and the can exploded. The stalactites of caramel sauce hanging from the ceiling would have done Steven Speilberg justice. The wife could see where he had tried to rub the sauce off with a dish cloth but all he had managed to do was to create an interesting caramel stucco effect on the ceiling. Now you've got to give this man full marks for ingenuity. When she walked right into the kitchen, she could see he was getting it off the ceiling in a very unique way. It was slow but it was working. The husband had found that their pet dog also liked the sauce so all he was doing was holding the dog up so he could slowly lick his way across the ceiling! Ten out of ten for problem solving.

The human mind is a bit like the earth — it grows what you put into it. Plant crops, it will grow crops. Plant weeds and it will grow weeds. Plant crops but neglect them and weeds will overtake them and strangle them. Think only negative thoughts and your actions reflect that negativity. Think positively and your life reflects your positive attitudes. Abraham Lincoln said 'Most people are about as happy as they make up their mind to be'. Norman Vincent Peale, the man who coined the phrase 'positive thinking', put it this way: **'Those who think they can and those who think they can't, are right.'**

Some years ago I was rushed to hospital with

intense pains in the chest. I thought it was a heart attack but it wasn't. It was malignant cancer in the lung. I nearly died twice and my wife and five young children came to the bedside to say goodbye. My eldest son, who is today a doctor, was just thirteen. My youngest was only six. I didn't die. The fact is I couldn't afford to. I had a huge mortgage on the house! As I walked out of the Prince Charles hospital four months later, two of the nursing sisters said: 'You were expected to die on two occasions and you didn't. We believe your mental attitude had a lot to do with that. It saved your life.' I also believe the skills of dedicated and talented doctors and medical staff plus the prayers of my family and friends made the significant difference. I was humbled to receive thousands of get well messages and simple notes saying, 'I'm praying for you.'

Dr Carl Simonton, director of the Cancer Counselling and Research Centre, Fort Worth, Texas, wrote these interesting words in his book *Getting Well Again*. 'The results of our approach to cancer treatment made us confident of this conclusion — a positive mental attitude participation can influence the onset of disease, the outcome of treatment and the quality of life.'

Research conducted at Pittsburgh Cancer Institute by psychologist Sandra Levy found that a factor called "joy" — a term used to describe mental resilience and vigour — was the second strongest factor in the survival of a group of women with recurring breast cancer. While I'm not suggesting that all cancer can be cured by meditation or positive attitude, these factors certainly do appear to help in coping with all sicknesses and diseases. I've never met a doctor or nurse yet who thinks they are an obstacle.

If you are interested in the role of the mind in healing, you ought to read Norman Cousins' book *Anatomy of an Illness*. Cousins, an American, was told he had about a one in five hundred chance of recovery from a crippling disease. To cut a long story short, he discharged himself from hospital and, with the aid of his doctor embarked on a unique form of self-treatment. He was in so much pain he couldn't sleep. To overcome that, he hired a movie projector and a heap of comedies. Cousins discovered that ten minutes of laughter somehow eased the pain enough to enable him to catch two hour's sleep. When the pain woke him, he went back to his comedies. Norman Cousins is alive and well and back at work.

It is claimed that the body releases natural chemicals called endorphins which are supposed to be even more powerful than morphine. They create a feeling of well-being and aid the body in its struggle to heal itself. Joggers talk about the feeling of well-being they experience through their jogging which also releases endorphins. The same feeling comes about through laughing. In an age of stress we need to laugh more, don't you think?

Dr Steven Locke, a psychiatrist at Beth Israel Hospital in Boston, believes the understanding of the relationship between mind and body could be the third revolution in Western medicine, ranking it with the advent of surgery and the discovery of penicillin.

One interesting observation about positive thinking: the human mind seems incapable of containing positive and negative thoughts at the same time. An old Japanese proverb says 'love and fear cannot eat out of the the same bowl' and it is the same with positive and negative attitudes; they don't fit comfortably in the one head. One final thing about positive thinkers: winners concentrate on their desires, not on their limitations. Here's a thought-provoking quote: 'What would you attempt to do if you knew you could not fail.' Isn't that a mind blower?

**'don't leave the development of your potential
to chance'**

Setting
Your Goals

What is a goal? A goal is an ambition, a dream, a desire you can define.

Maybe you are not into setting goals for your life. Perhaps you are frightened to set big goals because you might fail. You may have convinced yourself that one way to avoid the embarrassment of possible failure is never to start. But we all do set goals. You want to catch a bus at 10 am. You make sure you're at the bus stop a couple of minutes before. You may run late but you'll only do it a few times because, sooner or later, you'll get tired of missing the bus. Wanting to catch the bus will finally motivate you to organise yourself to be there in time to catch it. That's goal setting. If you want to eat tonight then you must buy some food today at the supermarket. That's goal setting. Goal setting is simply a matter of doing what is necessary to achieve what you want. We do it every day. As a matter of fact, you couldn't survive without unconscious goal setting.

When American motivator and businessman James Rohn was in my studio, he offered this sensible bit of advice: '**Don't leave the development of your potential to chance**.' Yet, for some peculiar reason, many of us do. We just wander through life with no plan, no goals, no idea of what we really want out of life, out of relationships, out of our marriages, out of our jobs. Occasionally a wonderful but rather vague idea comes into our heads about something we want to own or would like to achieve. We never get around to actually planning to do it. We never sit down and put anything on paper. We expect it to stay in our minds, forgetting that our minds are being bombarded with all the other daily demands of living. In many cases we just bounce from one crisis to another, lurching from one disaster to another. Is that your experience? I call that 'the pinball philosophy of life'.

You can easily identify the people who are into the pinball philosophy. They're the ones who are always talking about 'One day I'm gunna' or 'If only I'd'. An honest man by the name of James Albury once wrote the following epitaph for himself, to be placed on his gravestone:

> *'He slept beneath the moon,*
> *he baked beneath the sun;*
> *He lived a life of going to do,*
> *and died with nothing done.'*

I believe that life is an art, not an accident. We readily accept the fact that we have to learn to walk, learn to read, write, spell, do maths. We have to learn the skills and the rules for football, tennis, cooking, driving a car. What's more, if we want to be good at it, to make a success of it, we have to not only know it, we have to practise it constantly. If we want to do the best we can, we have to be willing to exercise, practise, sacrifice and concentrate on that goal more than anything else. In other words, what price are you willing to pay to achieve your goals? I'm fortunate in my job in radio because I meet so many interesting people and I learn from listening to them and observing them. I've never met a person who is making a success out of life who doesn't have a real sense of purpose and isn't committed to that purpose.

I believe you've got to be able to put your goals on paper. As a matter of fact, I think it's essential to put your goals on paper. You need to be able to define and explain each one in a simple sentence and they have to be worthwhile to command your respect. In doing this you set a pattern, you know where you are and what you are doing with your unique, one shot at life.

I remember interviewing Zig Ziglar, a well known American motivational speaker. Zig came up with a quote I've always remembered, '**There is no excitement in mediocrity.**' If you can't feel that your goals are worthwhile, you're going to have a hard job getting enthusiastic and convincing yourself that they are worth the time, effort and sacrifice it will require to achieve them. As a matter of fact, it is a good idea not only to put your goals down on paper, but also to be able to put down a reason for setting these goals.

A goal is the motivator, the inspiration for people on the way up. **Goals don't matter to people who are going nowhere** but for people who want to do something with their lives, goals are essential. I believe that the inability to establish goals is a major obstacle to success and achievement. Many people can't define their goals, they can't direct their activities and, as a result, their activities and their lives are aimless, lacking purpose and any sense of achievement.

Do you remember that great story from your childhood about Alice in Wonderland? Alice came to the fork in the road and said to the Cheshire Cat, 'Cat, which of these roads shall I take?' When the cat replied, 'Well, my dear, where do you want to go?' Alice said, 'I don't know.' So the cat's wise answer was, 'Then any road will do.' Zig Ziglar put it this way: 'There is no such thing as a favourable trade wind if you have no idea of where you are going.'

You wouldn't try to find a street in a strange town without some direction. You wouldn't build a house without a plan. You probably wouldn't even build a dog house without a plan. Yet so many of us lurch through life — our most valuable asset — and we have no plan. What a waste! What a tragedy! You don't need me to remind you that there will never be another day like today. There may be plenty of Mondays or Thursdays or Sundays but this is the only chance you get to use and enjoy this particular day. After midnight, it's gone. For good.

The poorest man on earth is the one without a dream. So start dreaming because goals come from dreams. I am always inspired when I read the story of Martin Luther King, the American preacher and civil rights campaigner whose dream was to see racial hatred and discrimination ended: 'I have a dream that one day this nation will rise up and live out the true meaning of its creed: "We hold these truths to be self-evident that all men are created equal." I have a dream that one day on the red hills of Georgia sons of former slaves and the sons of former slave owners will be able to sit down together at the table of brotherhood. I have a dream that my four little children will one day live in a nation where they will not be judged by the colour of their skin but by the content of their character. I have a dream today.'

If you haven't read all of that speech, get hold of it and read it. It will bring tears to your eyes, a sense of nobility to your heart, not to mention stimulation for your mind. Remember also as you read Martin Luther King's words, that you are reading something almost sacred. It was his dream. It was a dream for which he gave everything he had, including his life. Martin Luther King was assassinated in April 1968.

When you dream and then translate those dreams into goals you can strive towards, ask yourself how much it's going to cost you. Then ask yourself whether you are willing to pay the price.

A story is told about the ancient Greek philosopher Socrates who was allegedly standing near some water. A young man came to Socrates and asked him to help him find knowledge. Socrates grabbed the young man by the scruff of the neck and pushed his head underwater. Naturally the young man struggled and fought to get up. Just as he came up to gasp and gulp for air, Socrates pushed him under again. This went on a couple of times and finally when the young man was allowed to surface he looked with stunned disbelief at the great teacher and said 'Why did you do that?' Socrates is supposed to have replied, 'When you want knowledge as badly as you wanted air — you'll get it.'

I talk with lots of people who want someone else to do their thinking for them, do their decision making for them, live their lives for them, wave a magic wand and bestow the gift of self discipline, the gift of organising themselves, the gift of determination and will-power. They're the kind of people you meet everyday who say 'Why don't "they" do something about it? Why doesn't "somebody" take responsibility?' No one else can do these things for you. As with Socrates' young friend, 'when you want it enough, you'll get it!' The question is — what do you want and how much do you want it?

Dr Victor Frankl was a psychiatrist in Vienna, Austria, at the beginning of World War II. Like lots of people of Jewish ancestry, he was put into a German concentration camp, and, being a psychiatrist, he became interested in how some prisoners coped with life in the prison camp while others obviously couldn't. Only about one in twenty survived in places like Auschwitz. When Dr Frankl looked closely, he found that those prisoners with a sense of purpose, with something to live for, with goals, lived longer than those without purpose. Those with no goals lived in the past. They closed their eyes and life became meaningless.

Frankl made an interesting observation in his book *Man's Search for Meaning*: 'It is a peculiarity of man that he can only live by looking to the future.' Frankl also noted, 'Woe to him who saw no more sense in life, no aim, no purpose and therefore no point in carrying on. He was soon lost.' Jesus Christ said, 'If you want to find life, be prepared to lose it.' He wasn't suggesting you lose your life in a car accident. What he was talking about was losing or immersing your life in something bigger and greater than yourself. When you can do that, then you'll discover just how broad and deep and magnificent life can be. People like Mother Teresa of India, Martin Luther King, Albert Schweitzer and Ted Noffs of Sydney's Wayside Chapel are all illustrations of that truth. They have all found their lives enriched by 'losing' themselves in a challenge.

If you want to do something worthwhile with your life, start dreaming. Then convert the dreams into goals. After all, a goal is only a dream with a deadline. I sometimes wonder how many people die with noble dreams trapped inside minds frozen by fear and repressed by lack of confidence to at least give it a try.

Time magazine published the results of a Yale University study in which 1953 graduates from the university were interviewed and it was found that only three percent of them had written goals. Ten percent had a vague idea of some goals and eighty-seven percent had no specific goals at all. Twenty years after graduation, in 1973, researchers interviewed as many of the graduates as possible. The interesting things was that the three percent had achieved more, at least in financial terms, than the ninety-seven percent.

In recent times we've heard a lot about visualisation — constantly visualising or throwing up the picture of your goals on the screen of your mind until your goals become part of your subconscious mental process. The term 'visualising' may be new to some but the process isn't. We think in pictures. I notice that if I'm looking to buy a new car, I'm sensitive to just about every ad about cars, become interested in cars, buy the motoring magazines, go to the Motor Show that year but once I've made the decision, signed the paper and started driving the new car, I don't worry about cars until it's time to change again. If you talk about it with people, they will agree that we are sensitive to those things we are interested in. Visualising what you want to achieve is not going to make it happen, as if by magic; all visualising does is keep your goal active in your mind and your mind focussed on your goals. There will still be hard work to do but at least you'll know where you are heading in your life.

Practical Ideas
for Goal Setting

1. Write your goals down

Unless you are some kind of superhuman, I don't think dreams become realistic until you put them on paper. Then you start to get them into focus and you are making some sort of commitment or covenant with yourself. Dreams and desires that only float around in your mind can be so easily crowded out by all the other pressures that can hit you in the course of a day or week. I'm going to encourage you to make more than just one goal.

Many people I've talked with about goal setting

often make the mistake of having only one goal —
usually to do with career or finances. I think that's a
mistake because it creates a very narrow vision of
life and, consequently, a narrow person. I'm going
to suggest that you set goals in five other aspects of
your life as well. We'll deal with those areas a little
later. Can you run the risk of juggling these six areas
of goals in your thinking when there is so much to
compete with them? It's easier to put them down on
paper and carry that on you.

2. Make sure goals are positive

It's so easy to set a negative goal such as 'I'm not
going to smoke today' but, every time you think of
your goal, what does it remind you of? That's right,
a cigarette! In an attempt to give up, you are
constantly reminding yourself of your missed
smokes. You are more likely to succeed if you set a
positive goal — I'm getting a healthy body, tar-free
lungs, reducing the risk of cancer. That healthy,
positive outlook emphasises an attractive, constructive mental picture. The same technique works for
losing weight. It's not a case of saying I must give
up that cream bun — rather set yourself the goal of
a more attractive, fit body. The bun is no real
sacrifice when you want the goal more than the
calories and the spare tyre of fat hanging over your
belt! Make your goals positive and make them in
the present tense — I am getting a healthier body. I
am getting fitter.

3. Make your goals worthwhile

Goals need to be worthwhile to command your respect and your effort. There's a real sense of joy and achievement in gaining a goal that has demanded something of you. For a goal to be worthwhile you've got to want it with a passion. Forget it if all you can work up is a mild feeling of interest. If the best you can do is to say you would 'like' this or that, don't put it on your list. You need fire in your belly! If you need encouragement, read the biographies of some of the great reformers and the achievers. I remember once talking to the late Sir Reg Ansett. He started with one truck but owning one truck was not his ultimate goal — it was just a stepping stone. He wanted, worked for and got, a fleet of trucks, then buses, then aeroplanes to form Ansett Airlines.

4. Make your goals realistic

Other people are doing it. You can, too, if that's what you want but it's not realistic to start with nothing today and expect to achieve it by this time next week. Once you set your goal, you then have to devise your plan or strategy to achieve it and start putting it into a time frame. You may not be after money; you may want a University degree. You know that will take at least three or four years. In this case the time frame is set up for you by the university but in others no-one will set the timetable for you. You have to set your own. You have to make a commitment to persevere until you achieve what you want. No matter what the goal, set a realistic time limit and develop your working strategy for achieving it.

5. Make your goals specific

Don't say to yourself 'I want to save some money'. How much do you want to save? What do you want the money for? Be specific. Don't just say I want a car. What make? What model? Be specific. Don't say I want to go overseas on a holiday. Where do you want to go — what countries? What do you want to see? Get the booklets from your travel agents, work out a budget. Be specific.

> Don't rush your goal setting. Take your time. Get away on your own for the weekend and jot down your ideas, refining, adding, scrapping and changing your notes until you've got something on paper you can get excited about. I cannot stress too much the need to set goals that excite and challenge you. You need to do that to motivate yourself.

Sharing your goals with a close personal friend who is sympathetic and supportive can be extremely helpful. Sharing helps you to reduce your goals to concise, understandable sentences. It also means you've declared them, so you have something to live up to. I believe that's a large part of the success of many of the weight loss programs. People go along once a week and meet with other weight losers. In the sympathetic atmosphere people tell me they draw strength from the knowledge that others are also trying to achieve a similar goal.

I don't know if you know much about AA — Alcoholics Anonymous — that's the organisation for people who are having problems with alcohol. When they get to a point of desperation with their drinking and finally admit they've got a problem, they are taught by AA to set goals to help get them out of their mess. They are taught to get through the day without a drink. They are told not to worry about thinking about life without alcohol for a week, or a month or a year. They are encouraged just to get through one day at a time. If they're in such a mess that they can't even go one day without a drink, they're encouraged to set themselves the goal of going just one hour without a drink. If the going looks impossible they are encouraged to phone another AA member who will support and encourage them. Now that's goal setting — and it works!

The people in AA have a beautiful prayer: 'God grant me the serenity to accept the things I cannot change; the courage to change the things I can; and the wisdom to know the difference.'

By the way, there is no point sharing your goals with people who don't understand, who have no goals of their own or who think goal setting is a waste of time. Don't waste your time with those people.

A worthwhile exercise is to write down the date ten years from now and try to imagine where you will be, what you will be doing and what you will have achieved by that date. When you can see on paper what your mind visualises you will achieve in ten years' time, there is only one more question to ask yourself: 'What have I got to do to achieve that? There are some pages at the end of the book for that sort of exercise.

I meet plenty of people who have vague, unrealistic ideas floating around in their heads but they have never taken the trouble to clarify them and put them on paper. They have never asked themselves how much they want that goal, how much they're willing to pay to achieve it. Nor do they spend any time planning how they're going to achieve that goal. Maybe they think that, having thought of it, it will now drop into their laps from out of the blue. Sorry, it doesn't work like that.

The secret to success without work, is still a secret.

6. Plan your strategy

Writing down a goal won't make it happen. You've got to develop a working plan or strategy to achieve it. You go about planning a strategy as simply as planning a trip from A to B. Write down what you want and then plan a step-by-step approach to achieve it. Set yourself a timetable with a finishing date for your strategy. Deadlines may annoy you but they are valuable task masters.

Have you ever noticed how deadlines motivate you to get the job done? Let's imagine that you want to have something or be something, ten years from now. Start calculating what things you will have to do over the next ten years to achieve that. Break up the ten year project into bite-sized pieces.

A prize which is ten years away will take discipline to achieve but, if you are doing something every week which is helping you towards that goal, then you feel a sense of achievement and the goal is no longer remote. Calculate where you will need to be in five years' time, two years' time, one year's time to help keep you on target. Then break up that first year into quarters, months, and weeks. It is also important to sit down regularly and review your progress.

We can put this whole issue of goal setting into three simple questions:

1. Where am I?
2. Where do I want to go?
3. What have I got to do to achieve it?

If you set more than one goal, decide on their priorities, so you give most attention to the most important, not the easiest. You may need to do some research to reach your goal. Maybe you will need to talk to experts to get there. You may have to work with some other people to achieve. Get organised. A proverb in the Bible reads, 'He that walks with wise men, shall be wise' and it's my experience that successful people are willing to share their experiences with you and can provide inspiration and encouragement.

Some people set "Smart" goals. That is, they are Specific, Measurable, Achievable, Realistic and have a Timetable.

COMMITMENT:

1. I will write my goals down
2. I will make them positive
3. I will make my goals worthwhile
4. I will make my goals realistic
5. I will make my goals specific
6. I will plan my strategy

Signature:_____

'time is the scarcest resource and unless it is managed, nothing else can be managed'

Being Realistic

It's not only important to set the goals and devise a strategy to achieve them, it's also important to give some thought to what obstacles you might encounter on the way. It's a bit like packing your bag for holidays. You consider possible needs and plan for them. What obstacles could stand in your way to prevent you achieving your goals? One of the obvious obstacles could be lack of money. So you'll have to put that on the obstacle list — not to let it intimidate you but rather to find a solution. Perhaps your family, husband or wife don't share your goal and you feel that their understanding is important — you will have to work on that obstacle.

They may ridicule your plans but don't let that stop you, rather do some mental preparation to cope with that. What can you do to get rid of those obstacles? If you can't remove them or go over them, you can go around them. It's a good idea to jot down what you will do if you meet obstacles on the way.

1. Consider your weaknesses

As well as obstacles, it's also important to recognise your own strengths and weaknesses. We are all happy to think and talk about what strengths we may have but often we brush off admitting our weaknesses in case that appears like negative thinking. It's not negative, it's realistic. I have a friend who is wonderfully creative but he has a blind spot when it comes to organising money and this causes him a lot of problems. The positive thing to do about this is to recognise the problem and face up to it. He did that and now an accountant looks after that area of his business. It does several things for him. It relieves him of the stress and anxiety, it improves his credibility and reputation in the business community and it frees him to spend more time being creative.

When you are planning your strategy to achieve your goals, be realistic about yourself because in that way you are being positive and solving problems before they arise. However, a word of warning here: recognising your weaknesses is not negative but being obsessed and overwhelmed by them is. Being so overcome by your weaknesses that you are too paralysed by fear to even have a go is negative. Facing up to your weaknesses and doing something about them is both positive and realistic. List your weaknesses just as Benjamin Franklin did and decide what you can do and will do to deal with them.

2. Set yourself a timetable

Don't just set a timetable — stick to it. Read that timetable regularly during the day, particularly last thing at night before bed and first thing in the morning. Put it up somewhere so you can see it. If necessary, make several copies of it to give yourself reminders. I'm reminded of the man who had a particularly memorable and emotional experience. He was so overawed by the occasion that he wrote it down on a piece of paper and whenever he had visitors he asked his wife to go to the attic and fetch his 'memorable event'. He would then read it to his friends. Imagine his feelings when one day his wife came back down stairs with a few tattered remnants of paper to tell him the mice had eaten his blessed experience. So if you are going to the trouble to work out a timetable for yourself, make a couple of copies — just in case one gets lost or the mice eat it!

If you're saving for a car, put up a picture of it to remind yourself. If you're planning an overseas trip, get some brochures, cut out some photos and put them up as reminders. That type of incentive is encouraging.

Do you remember when you were a youngster, playing with a magnifying glass? The sun didn't burn much until you brought it into focus. Maybe, like me, you used to hold a piece of paper in one hand and move the glass until there was just an intense spot of light focussed on the paper. It wasn't long before the paper started to burn. So too with goals. Get them into focus and keep them in focus.

Frances Chadwick, the first woman to swim the English Channel, quit the swim on her first attempt, just three miles from the French coast line. Apparently, there was a thick fog making visibility impossible. Chadwick's words, when she found out how close she had been to her goal were, 'If I could have seen France, I would have made it.'

If a timetable is a new idea for you and you find it hard to discipline yourself to follow it, don't be disappointed if you fail the first few times. Make sure your timetable is reasonable and realistic. Don't make it too demanding at first. Get used to the idea of working to a time schedule. Whatever you do, persevere and don't give up. History is full of success stories and often in these stories one factor turns the incident from failure to success. That factor is perseverance. I believe perseverance is more important than talent, more important than education. Perseverance is the quality that keeps you hanging on, sometimes by your finger tips, when you are longing to give up.

Our society isn't too keen on enduring pain or discomfort; we are inclined to choose the soft, comfortable, easy way. Nevertheless, the athletes who break the records, the students seeking their best results and the businessmen striving to achieve seldom succeed by taking the soft option. Invariably it is through perseverance and endurance that the goal is achieved.

Calvin Coolidge, the thirtieth President of the United States, wrote: 'Nothing in the world can take the place of persistence. Talent will not; nothing is more common than unsuccessful men with talent. Genius will not; unrewarded genius is almost a proverb. Education alone will not; the world is full of educated derelicts. Persistence and determination alone are omnipotent.'

If you have trouble persevering, set worthwhile goals for yourself — goals that will excite you and challenge you. Perseverance is just another word for wanting. But it is often a wanting until it hurts, a wanting that just refuses to give up.

3. Take a tough attitude to the organisation of your time

Benjamin Disraeli, once Prime Minister of England said, 'the secret of success is constancy of purpose'. He who manages time, manages life because time is the precious resource we need to make a life for ourselves. Set goals which will inspire you, keep your eyes on those goals, and that will motivate you to enthusiastic action and the most productive management of your time. In *How to be an Effective Executive*, Peter Drucker notes that '**time is the scarcest resource and unless it is managed, nothing else can be managed**'.

It may not have occurred to you that when it comes to time, we are all born and treated equally. The world's top sportsmen and women, the world's wealthiest men and women, the achievers of our generation, the people we regard as successful, have exactly the same number of hours, minutes and seconds as we have. *The difference is how we use them.*

Benjamin Franklin commented about time: 'Do you love life? Then do not waste time, because that is the stuff that life is made of.' A seventh century Muslim leader, Omar Al Halif, said, '**Four things come not back: the spoken word, the sped arrow, time past, and the neglected opportunity**.' Many people have difficulty organising their time but I think a lot of this is negative self talk. We convince ourselves that time is hard to organise so we make sure it is, if only to prove ourselves right. It is essential to burn into your mind the simple truth that time not used effectively is gone and can't be re-used at some other time when you've got the energy or the inclination. We cannot march up to the timekeeper at the end of the month and say 'I wasted time on the 5th, 14th and 23rd. I'd like to get that time back now because there are things that need doing and I could use that time very effectively.' It doesn't work that way does it?

Organising time is usually based on a decision whether the job to be done is important or urgent, enjoyable or difficult. If it is enjoyable, we seldom have trouble facing up to it. If it is difficult, unpleasant, boring, threatening or likely to cause embarrassment or stress, we will go to incredible lengths to put it off, delay it, forget it or ignore it. We'll put it on the bottom of the list. We may even get around to making a phone call and then breathing a sigh of relief when the person we have to talk to isn't in.

We often deal with things that are urgent simply because they have become urgent. If we had dealt with them when we should have, they wouldn't be urgent now. William James: 'Nothing is so fatiguing as the eternal hanging on of an uncompleted task.' Often we spend time doing things that are urgent when we should be doing things that are more important. Some people get to like the buzz of urgency — they enjoy the adrenalin rush. It can easily give you the impression that you are important, doing significant things. It can also be an indicator that you can't organise your breakfast.

Psychologists often talk about Type A behaviour. Type A people are always frantically trying to beat the clock, trying to squeeze more and more activity into less and less time. However, they are not necessarily good workers. They may think they are movers and shakers but, in fact, many of them are poor time organisers. Type A behaviour is a significant contributor to stress, anxiety and heart disease. The answer is not so much to work harder but to work smarter.

4. Plan tomorrow, tonight

Dr Norman Vincent Peale once told me to plan my tomorrow, tonight. Don't go to bed until you have made notes tonight about the things you want to do tomorrow, who you want to call, who you want to see, who you want to write to. Many of us don't do that. We waste the first valuable and productive time of the morning getting organised. Dr Peale pointed out that many of us can't get to sleep at night because our minds are buzzing with all the thoughts of the day just past and the plans for the next day. What we should do is get it down on paper so that it doesn't interrupt our sleep. He suggests that, just as we take off our day clothes, so we ought to undress our minds, discarding all the cares and worries of the day, so we can relax and get really beneficial sleep and rest.

Even though time is such a scarce resource, that doesn't mean we shouldn't relax. Relaxing, going for a walk, spending quality time with family and friends, going on vacation: these are not only worthwhile uses of time, they are essential. Setting aside a time each day for creative thinking is a very important use of time. How can I improve myself? How can I improve my career chances? How can I better my relationships with my family? Creative thinking is planning for the future. Some people are so busy getting through today they feel they haven't got time to plan for the future. That's short-sighted. After all, if you are going on a journey, you give some thought to what you will need to make it enjoyable and successful. How much money will I need? What about the ticket, a passport, what sort of clothing and so on? Planning for the future is no different. Lack of planning is simply making tomorrow harder for ourselves than it needs to be.

Some people I talk with think planning and goal setting is all too much trouble. In fact, not planning makes life tougher, not easier because it's a bit like trying to build a house without a plan. Other people adopt the laid-back approach that they are the victims of life — that what will be, will be and they have no control. That's not my observation or experience. As I see it, it's like two rafts on a river — one with a rudder and an engine, the other with no steering and no power. I know which one I'd rather be on. Charles Kettering said, **'We should all be concerned about the future because we will have to spend the rest of our lives there.'**

While you can't get more than twenty-four hours into each day or more than sixty minutes into each hour, it is possible to make more effective use of time. Former US, President Herbert Hoover, wrote a book in the time he spent waiting at railway stations. If you arrive at a restaurant a little before your guest, you can use small blank cards you carry in your pocket to jot down a few notes or thoughts.

Do you realise that if you got up an hour earlier each day and devoted that time to the study of a specific subject, you would virtually be adding a month of useful time to each year? Think about that — thirteen months in the year!

5. Calculate the cost

Achieving your goal will cost you something. If it costs nothing, it's probably worth nothing. You may have to make sacrifices. You may have to study while others are relaxing. You may have to work while others are taking it easy. You may have to save while others are spending their money like there is no tomorrow. Australia's great tennis player, Evonne Cawley (formerly Evonne Goolagong) said, 'Whenever I felt I might be missing something, I reminded myself that this is what I had to do to get ahead in tennis. I would be giving up some things to get what I wanted most.'

Charles du Bos said: '**The important thing is this — to be able at any moment to sacrifice what we are for what we could become.**' A concert violinist gave a brilliant solo performance and afterwards a gushing member of the audience rushed up to him to compliment him on his skill and talent. 'I'd give half my life to play like that,' said the listener. The violinist replied, ' I did.'

When you have set your goals, ask yourself what the possible cost could be. Then ask yourself if you are willing to pay the price. That way, when you think you have to make some sacrifice, it doesn't come as a shock and you are prepared. A wit once said 'If you think it's expensive — wait till you get the bill for not trying.'

Just a word about self-discipline. It's not as hard as we sometimes think. If I'm about to cross the road and I see a car coming, my brain tells my leg muscles to wait a minute before stepping off the curb. That's self-discipline; the mind controlling my actions in the interest of an admirable cause — survival. Self-discipline is simply the mind (in this case inspired by my fascination with survival) taking control to achieve something it considers important. When we say we 'lack self-discipline' what we really mean is that we haven't yet come to the point of giving our goal the importance it needs to motivate us.

COMMITMENT

1. I will consider my weaknesses
2. I will set myself a timetable
3. I will take a tough attitude on the organisation of my time
4. I will plan tomorrow tonight
5. I will calculate the cost

Signature:_____

Six Areas for Goal Setting

You may have failures but don't be distracted. Let them serve only as learning experiences. I believe I actually learn more from my failures than I do from my successes. If I do something successfully, I don't analyse it as carefully as if I didn't succeed. Let me illustrate. In high school I was active in athletics and football. If I won a race or played a good game, I seldom tried to work out why it had been a winner but, if I ran badly or played badly, I always stopped to ask myself why.

It is also true, that successes generate more successes because they develop confidence. Knowing we

can do something we are more willing to try a
second or third time, hence the saying 'Nothing
succeeds like success'.

However, don't rest on your past successes. Don't
put things off. Be methodical and self-disciplined.
Be prepared to pay the price to achieve your goals.
Asked the secret of his success, Thomas Edison said
it was five percent inspiration and ninety-five
percent perspiration! Stick with your goal until it
becomes a reality. Reward yourself along the way. A
recent study suggests that people wanting to lose
weight had most success when they rewarded
themselves during their weight loss program — not
with a cream bun of course but maybe a record,
book or movie.

A word of warning here: you may set a goal or goals
and then decide to change your goals down the
track because your sense of direction has changed.
That's fine; set new goals and don't feel guilty. This
is different from dropping your goals because you
feel lazy and you're unwilling to have a go.
However, those goals which, on reflection later in
life, don't fit in with your maturing and changing
values or standards should not be changed or
dropped unless you are replacing them with better
ones.

At the age of thirty, spending time with your family
may become important. The goal set as a young
single man may need to be modified because, at

twenty a family may not have appeared so important. Service to the community may become a significant and satisfying part of your life. You may have to make changes to your goals to accommodate this new experience. I've met people who have made fame or money a goal and have pursued that objective relentlessly, with incredible singleness of purpose. They've achieved their goals but missed out on the satisfaction of a family's love or a community's appreciation.

A man who is always a welcome visitor to my studio is businessman and adventurer Dick Smith. Dick tells me he wasn't a brilliant student at school. When he left at the age of fifteen, he worked in a repair shop fixing taxi radios. He saw the opportunity to open a shop selling spare parts and electronic bits and pieces for the hobbyists and built an empire of electronic stores all over Australia and sold out to retire as a millionaire. He was the first man to fly a helicopter solo around the world. He started the *Australian Geographic* magazine, in spite of the negative voices who told him it wouldn't work. He has become involved in promoting and organising Life Education Centres throughout Australia. One day, when Dick was flying his helicopter over some bushland, he recognised an area where he had gone bushwalking as a youngster. He had often thought of those times and wished he could go back bushwalking but like so many people, he kept telling himself he was too busy. Instead of regretting his lost moments of bushwalking, he reorganised his time so he, his wife Pip and their children could once again go bushwalking. Dick is a classic case of the man who has changing and expanding goals.

You have to decide what is important to you: so your values and standards will influence your goal setting.

When setting goals, don't think just in terms of money, career, house, car, overseas trip, personal jet and so on. Careers and finances are important but so also are the other areas of our lives — our families, our social relationships with others. Add to those goals the need to set some goals for our personal lives — our health and physical well being, the improvement of our minds and the development of our spiritual lives. I recognise that some people shy away from the suggestion that our spiritual development is important. Anything 'spiritual' is confused by some with 'religion' and I can understand people shying away from formal, organised religion. In some people's opinions 'religion' has had a pretty shabby history but I also believe we owe much of our progress in civilisation to the dedicated work of people who allowed the spiritual side of their natures to dignify and elevate their minds and lives. As a result, unselfish and noble in service, they enriched the lives of millions.

For my part, I feel I need to think about God with other like-minded people at our local church — and

I enjoy it. My church is not perfect, neither are the people, including myself, who go there. Dr Billy Graham told a story about a young man looking for the perfect wife. Unfortunately, when he found her, she was looking for the perfect husband. Some people can never find a suitable church because they are looking for the perfect church that suits their every whim and desire. They seldom find it.

A lot of people neglect the spiritual area of their lives. You may neglect it but I believe it is there, nevertheless. I'm convinced that humans are more than intelligent, talking animals. Wayne Dyer, author of *Your Erroneous Zones* and a number of other excellent books, made this point during an interview: 'We are not so much human beings having a spiritual experience, but spiritual beings having a human experience.'

Start reading, thinking and searching for spiritual truth. If you are stuck for ideas, start with the simple teachings of Jesus — not necessarily any particular person's or church's view of those teachings but the real thing. Get hold of an easily read version, such as the *Good News Bible*, and read the simple but moving story of Jesus and his teachings from any of the accounts by Matthew, Mark, Luke or John.

After all, aren't most people really yearning for happiness, serenity and peace of mind? All of these are spiritual qualities.

If you have difficulty with the Christian faith, don't close your mind to the idea of spiritual discovery. Go to a library or a bookshop and browse until you find something you believe is worthy of your attention.

Get a sheet of paper, write down the following six areas and start setting goals in each one:

1. Career objectives
2. Financial needs
3. People — family life and social experiences
4. Mental growth
5. Spiritual discoveries
6. Physical health

Such an outline will help you make sure your goals don't clash. Goals need to complement each other and function in your life like cogs in a machine. Furthermore, there is little point setting financial or career goals that eliminate time for family, social life and physical health.

What's the difference between goal setting and the old New Year's Resolution? Serious, life-changing goal setting requires a daily commitment and a continuing determined action to pursue those goals.

Above all, take responsibility for your own life. Don't sit around blaming others for your misfortunes or your inability to achieve something worthwhile with your life. That's one of the greatest excuses of all times and lots of people do it. Once we have set our goals, we can get on with improving our performance, stretching our minds, and developing our abilities. You may even be fifty or sixty and have no goals for yourself. With time marching on — it's all the more important for you to do it.

Goals are great but so is the journey. As a matter of fact, I sometimes think the journey is every bit as much fun as the achievement of the goal. I look on life as a journey. I have more than one goal so it's an ongoing experience moving from one goal, one destination to another. After all, it would be a boring old trip if only the goal counted. Arriving at your anticipated destination is a lot more fun, more exciting and more stimulating if you can look out the window and enjoy the journey as well as the arrival.

Life really is exciting. There is so much to learn, so much to experience and discover. Be on the look out for opportunities to learn. There are so many good books to read, tapes to listen to, study courses to do, videos to watch, to help you improve your enjoyment of life and your personal performance. Charlie 'Tremendous' Jones, the delightfully enthusiastic speaker from America, has a great saying about life. One day when he was chatting in the studio he said, *'You are the same today as you'll be in five years except for two things, the people you meet and the books you read.'*

You know what I enjoy so much about reading? It's not so much the information I get out of the book, it's the mental stimulation triggering off new ideas that sometimes take me miles away from the book's topic, stretching my mind and leading me into fresh territory and new ventures. The best way to consolidate that learning is to have a journal handy. Every time you hear or see a good quote or a good idea, jot it down in your journal. When you are reading, keep the journal beside you because even a sentence or phrase from a work of fiction can be worth noting. When you go to a lecture, take your journal. It doesn't have to be anything expensive. A simple school notebook will do. I have a couple of journals, one in my briefcase, one at home and one in my office. Every few months I go through them and take the material out of the journal, sorting it into classifications or groups and put it all on computer disk for future reference. There is no point in keeping a journal if you don't browse over the material regularly. A young friend of ours went to study overseas for a year. He knew he would be homesick so he took some old journals to help him relive his home experiences. At the same time he reminded himself of some of the greatest lessons he had learned.

Getting Motivated, Staying Motivated

Making a new resolution is relatively easy. To change your attitude for a day or two or to set goals and be really keen about them for a while is fairly simple. But how do you maintain your enthusiasm, not just for a couple of days but for weeks, months, even years? To do this we need to really understand what enthusiasm is.

The word enthusiasm comes from two Greek words — 'en' meaning 'in' and 'theos' meaning 'god'. It literally means "god possessed" and, if you've ever met someone who is enthusiastic, that's a fairly good description. An enthusiastic person lights up

135

when he talks about his favourite subject. Just listen
to the change in the tone of voice when they're on
their pet topic — they behave like someone
possessed! The voice gets a new ring of excitement,
the eyes light up, the face becomes animated.

Try an experiment sometime: get a friend talking on
their favourite subject — whether it's fishing,
football, their new car, a flower, politics or some
cause they believe in. Study the face, listen to the
voice, catch the excitement, the joy and the conviction and you'll know what enthusiasm is about.

One of the interesting things about enthusiasm is
that it doesn't cost a cent. You don't have to come
from a wealthy family to enjoy it. You don't have to
be highly educated to possess it. It is also highly
contagious. It is the essential quality of leadership,
and every successful person I've ever met possesses
it. Ralph Waldo Emerson said: **'Nothing great was
achieved without enthusiasm.'**

The interesting thing about enthusiasm is that it
generates energy. I've never met a lazy, indifferent,
apathetic, negative thinking enthusiast. The human
mind just doesn't seem capable of possessing
positive, happy, enthusiastic thoughts and negative
thoughts at the same time.

So how do you become enthusiastic?

We get enthusiastic about the things we care about.

If you want to generate enthusiasm in your own life, start doing a little creative dreaming then bring those dreams down to earth and start turning them into worthwhile, reachable, attainable goals. Robert Kennedy quoted the words of George Bernard Shaw at the funeral of his brother, John F. Kennedy: 'Some men see things as they are and say "why?" Others dream things that never were and say "why not?"'

I once interviewed a young Englishman by the name of Robert Swan. At the age of twenty-eight and with no previous experience, he led an expedition to Antarctica. Once he got there, he took off with two companions each pulling a sled weighing 160 kilograms. They trudged through 1413 kilometres of icy Antarctic wastes and walked in the footsteps of the great explorer Captain Robert Scott to the South Pole. It took them seventy-one days. That was significant enough in itself. However, what captured my admiration was the story leading up to that magnificent achievement. I asked him how he got started, what had given him the idea to tackle this huge challenge. He was refreshingly honest.

After leaving high school, he realised that he was going nowhere and doing nothing with his life. At the age of eighteen he was also drinking too much.

Robert decided to do something worthwhile and that's when he decided to walk in the steps of Scott. With what little money he had, he rented a warehouse in London and with a phone as his only asset, he started asking people for support, donations and sponsorship. He soon ran out of money — he worked as a labourer, gardener, waiter — whatever job he could get but he never lost his enthusiasm or his determination. He plodded on for ten years until he was ready to lead a team of experienced people on the expedition. He was not only the leader, he was also the youngest and the only inexperienced member of the team.

They ran into a number of difficulties and disasters, including the loss of their ship, the "Southern Quest". They also lost money on the venture. But Robert Swan didn't walk away from the project. He set off around the world talking about it, doing interviews, showing slides and films, slowly repaying his debts, keeping faith with his financial backers. I remember one quote from our conversation: 'Anything is possible if you believe in what you are doing, if you make the effort to work, work, work to make things happen.'

I'm not sure that I would make walking to the South Pole a goal for my life. As an achievement for my life it doesn't excite me. Nevertheless, the last time I talked with Robert Swan he was planning his next venture — he was planning to walk to the North Pole. I never doubted his commitment. In May of 1989 Robert conquered that target — he had walked to the North Pole. He is believed to be the only man in history to have walked to both Poles. That's what I call enthusiasm!

Getting Motivated, Staying Motivated

Here are five ideas to help you stay motivated.

1. Keep your enthusiasm on the boil

I remember a college lecturer once telling us to 'get on fire — other people will come to watch you burn'. It's true, isn't it? The enthusiast is invariably the leader. Other people want his company, his warmth, his infectious optimism, his sense of purpose and direction. If you have the choice between playing on a team where there is enthusiasm and a team where there is none, I know which one I would choose. If you have to make a choice between two companies to work for, one which is enthusiastic and progressive and the other stodgy and lacking fire, which would you choose?

A story is told about a local church that caught fire. I'm afraid it was a rather dreary, unexciting place. The local neighbours turned out to watch the blaze. When the minister saw someone in the crowd who hadn't been to the church, he couldn't resist the opportunity to get in a commercial. 'First time I've seen you at church,' he said. His potential member replied, 'First time I've seen any fire in it.'

Setting goals gives you a target. Seeing that target in front of you keeps your enthusiasm on the boil. Writing those goals on to small cards and keeping them in your pocket, in your diary or by your bedside is an effective reminder of your commitment. Read them every morning and every night.

Recite them to yourself during the day.

Because there are many negative influences in our lives, such as bad news and gloomy, pessimistic people, I believe you have to take positive and determined steps to counteract them. You will have noticed throughout the book the frequent use of quotations. I find these one sentence gems of wisdom like a daily mind vitamin. Copy one on a card and keep it near you for the day. Refer to it frequently until it is stored in your subconscious mind and becomes part of your mind power resources. Keep your eyes open for more quotes and jot them down in your journal. Read other books on self-improvement, listen to tapes and go to seminars.

Keep reminding yourself that you are the owner of a unique life — the only one of its kind in history and it is yours to explore, to develop and to tackle worthwhile goals and dreams. Who can begin to guess the incredible potential of what you have? Anyone can tell the number of seeds in one apple. But who can begin to guess the number of apples in one seed? So it is with your life and mine.

2. Feed your enthusiasm with other people's successes

I suggest that for two reasons. First, it reminds you that it is possible for people to achieve goals and that encourages you to keep going after your goals.

Adopt the positive attitude — if he can do it, I can do it. Second, recognising other people's successes helps you to remain a generous person. I find a mean spirit in some people who resent other people's achievements. Anyone would think there is room for only one successful person in the world. If someone else is fortunate, don't say resentfully 'he was lucky', because I've noticed that the harder you work, the luckier you get! Be a generous person. Be an encourager. The day will come when you will also appreciate someone recognising and sharing your success.

3. Don't be slowed down by critics

The world is full of knockers. For every dreamer there must be at least ten critics. Where would we be if men like Edison, Columbus, Galileo and all the other great pioneers had listened to their critics? We'd still be back in the caves, contemplating our navels! I've never seen a statue erected to a critic. I've seen statues erected to pioneers, to those who have given generously of their lives to the community or laid down their lives in time of war to defend their nation. I've seen statues for scientists, inventors, even a dog — but I've never seen one for a critic!

Thomas Edison invented the record player, the electric locomotive, the microphone, a method for constructing concrete buildings, a device for producing sheet metal, a telegraph signal box and, of course, the light globe. The interesting thing is that at one stage members of his family tried to get him committed to a mental institution because of his obsession with inventing things. Edison's persistence was legendary.

4. Tackle something you don't want to do

Nothing fuels your enthusiasm like a success — however small that success may seem. One of the simplest ways I know to feel a real sense of achievement is to tackle something you don't want to do. Winston Churchill, the inspiring Prime Minister of Great Britain during World War II said, 'One ought never to turn one's back on a threatened danger and try to run away from it. If you do that, you will double the danger. But if you meet it promptly and without flinching, you will reduce the danger by half. Never run away from anything. Never!' Mastering our own wills is one of the greatest challenges for people interested in self-development. So much else depends on it. If others can do it, so can we.

5. Start the day with a good attitude

Some people roll out of bed and say, 'Oh no, not another work day.' But have you noticed they don't feel that way if they're waking up to go on holidays? We don't feel that way if we're waking up to find birthday or Christmas presents at the foot of the bed. We only feel bad about getting out of bed, if our attitude to the day is wrong. If there is something to look forward to, there's good reason to get out. If you thought you were getting out of bed to go on a long planned overseas trip, you'd have no trouble diving out of bed. If you were going to take delivery of your new car, would you find getting out of bed a struggle? If you knew that today the boss was going to announce your promotion to the position you've been working to achieve, would it be hard to go to work? Not likely. So what is there to look forward to tomorrow morning? The new day offers you another opportunity to work towards your exciting, challenging set of goals. That's great! That is exciting! So let yourself get enthusiastic.

A really positive thought to start the day is this one: 'Today is the first day of the rest of my life.' So many people make mistakes, have failures and then think it's all over, there is no second chance and they've blotted their copy book. Not so. That was yesterday. This is today, with all its fresh promise and new opportunities. Today is the only day you can live. You certainly can't live yesterday or tomorrow. Back in 65 BC Horace wrote:

> *Happy the man — and happy he alone*
> *Who can call today his own;*
> *Who, secure within, can say*
> *Tomorrow, do your worst — for I have lived today.*

I find it helpful to remind myself of the words written by the psalmist David: 'This is the day the

Lord has made, let us rejoice and be glad in it.' I have my own translation for that — 'This is the day God has made, I'm going to enjoy it and do my best.' That's called a positive affirmation. It's good also to be able to affirm at the end of the day — this was the day God made, I enjoyed it and I did do the best I could.

It will also pay you to find five or ten minutes every day to spend a few quiet moments in thought, making a list of things to be thankful for. It's easy to miss the good things because they are often gentle, subtle and not screamingly obvious but there are always things to be thankful for. Realising that can help significantly to get your eyes off your complaints and lift your enthusiasm.

COMMITMENT

1. I will keep my enthusiasm on the boil.
2. I will feed my enthusiasm with other people's successes.
3. I will ignore the negative critics.
4. I will tackle something I don't want to do.
5. I will start the day with a good attitude.

Signature:_____

'the mind is like a clock that is constantly running down; it has to be wound up daily with good thoughts'

Getting the Most Out of Your Life

If you want to get the most out of each day, keep reminding yourself of the need to live one day at a time. If you've done something in the past (yesterday) that bothers you so that you feel guilty or sorry, then put it right — apologise, fix it, whatever. My suggestion is that, if you are feeling bad about what you've said or done or haven't done you will feel better if you put it right. Otherwise, it will nag away in the back of your mind and give you no peace. If you're not prepared to fix it or you are convinced you can't fix it — and sometimes, unfortunately, past mistakes cannot be fixed — then the realistic thing is to be honest with yourself, recognise it, come to a point of accepting the fact, learn from the experience, close the book on the incident and get on with your life. If you are worried about the future (tomorrow) then don't bury your head in the sand. Take positive, sensible steps to get organised. If you're not prepared to, then stop stewing your insides worrying. Learn to live one day at a time. It takes the stress out of worrying about yesterdays and tomorrows.

If we believe that life is worth living, our belief will help create the fact. Remember what Menninger said: 'attitudes are more important than facts'.

A friend of mine had a nervous breakdown. He is a talented, intelligent and successful professional but he was a long time getting over the shattering experience. I've got no doubt his recovery would have been quicker if he had had something to live for, a sense of purpose, goals. Quite a lot of people run out of steam because they lack purpose in their lives. Bernard Russel, the English philosopher, once wrote: 'Continuity of purpose is one of the most essential ingredients of happiness'.

I find myself working on a number of projects at a time. They fall into the six categories mentioned in the section on goal setting. It may be something that can be achieved with a phone call or it may take weeks or even years to finalise. By having a number of projects there is always something to do, always something to achieve, to enjoy and to look forward to. **'The mind is like a clock that is constantly running**

down; it has to be wound up daily with good thoughts', said Bishop Fulton Sheen.

Enthusiasm is the key to leadership. It is the basic ingredient in a healthy mind. It is the seed from which come visions of the future. It is the inspiration of pioneers and the backbone of reformers — and we need it, lots of it, in every country in the world. One of the reasons I believe the nations of the Western World have lost their way is that they have lost any sense of the destiny of mankind. We live for the moment and the passing pleasure of the moment. Many great nations don't seem to have any goals. Their politicians can only see as far as the next election. We need leaders who can look beyond, to the future, to making the plans, setting the goals and creating a world for our children and our children's children for generations to come. We'll never get politicians like that until the people who vote for them have that same sense of destiny and vision.

We need that sense of vision and enthusiasm in our personal lives, in our homes, schools, universities, jobs, businesses, unions and parliaments. Who knows, with a little effort from everyone, some of that magic we call enthusiasm may spill over into this tense, tired and angry old world of ours and make it better. When you think about it, it really is a marvellous world after all. What it becomes is entirely up to us — you and me, nobody else.

Isn't it worth your best effort?

'a journey of a thousand miles must begin with a single step'

The Fifth Step

Be sure of one thing — life can be wasted.

The waste lies in the love we have but never give; in the wasted talents and abilities we have but never use. The waste is caused by the small-minded, selfish insecurity which will risk nothing. In wanting the easy way, the painless way, we are unwilling to make a sacrifice or to pay for what we want and so we miss out on happiness as well.

Life can be wasted because we fail to realise that we possess a unique life experience that no one else can live. It is ours and ours alone.

151

Power to Choose

It's not enough to just read and think about the ideas talked about in this book. The important thing is to start, to take the first step.

At the beginning of the book we talked about the four qualities — self-esteem, attitude, goal setting and motivation. I said then that we would leave the fifth till later. The fifth quality is the courage to act, the willingness to try.

The Chinese philosopher Lao Tzu, who lived about 500 BC, had a beautiful saying: **'A journey of a thousand miles must begin with a single step.'**

The fifth step is deciding to exercise the Power to Choose and deciding to do it right now.

Confidential Personal Progress Planner

Don't put the book down yet. You have some assessing and planning to do.

The following pages are set aside for your use to decide just where you are in your journey and to help you plan for the future. Use the pages that follow as your own personal plans or copy them and fill them out. We all have only the one life — give it all you've got!

There is an old Zen saying: 'To know and not to do is not yet to know.'

ON SELF-ESTEEM

Do I feel good about myself?

If the answer is no, why? What is causing that feeling?

What sort of self-image do I have of myself? Write down in a couple of sentences an honest description of how I think about myself.

Where did my self image come from? Describe some of the negative and positive experiences and influences that helped to shape it.

What sort of self image would I like to have? Come on, pluck up courage and write down in a couple of sentences a description of the person you would like to be.

What have I got to do to achieve it?

ON ATTITUDE

Am I a negative thinker? Is my first response to a situation or problem a negative one?

In what way do I respond negatively?

Why do I respond negatively?

What can I do about it?

What am I going to do about it?

ON GOAL SETTING

List at least three goals you want to work on in each of the six areas of your life.

1. CAREER

2. FINANCES

3. FAMILY AND SOCIAL

4. MENTAL

5. SPIRITUAL

6. PHYSICAL

Check to be certain that your goals are positive, worthwhile, realistic and specific. Are they exciting enough to challenge your enthusiastic effort? What about a timetable? Set a date for achieving each of your eighteen goals. Think about it carefully. Don't set the same date for all of them — you may bust a valve! It's important to spread your goals so that, when you achieve one, there is always another and then another to pursue. That helps to keep the excitement in your day and to keep you motivated.

HERE'S A FUN EXERCISE

Imagine or visualise yourself ten years from today. Don't rush your answers and don't put down the first thing that comes into your head. Really try to imagine yourself ten years down the track.

1. What is the date (ten years from now)?

2. What's my address?

3. My age?

4. Occupation?

5. What's my income?

6. Write a sentence or two describing the family.

7. Describe my social life.

8. What have I achieved in the area of my mental life?

9. What's happened in my spiritual life over ten years?

10. Describe my greatest achievement over the past ten years.

'what would you attempt to do if you knew you
could not fail?'

ANOTHER FUN EXERCISE

For the moment forget the goals you set a couple of pages back. Now working on the quote: 'What would you attempt to do if you knew you could not fail?', ask yourself what you would attempt in the six goal areas of your life believing you could achieve them. Write them down, taking your time.

1. Career

2. Finances

3. Family and Social

4. Mental

5. Spiritual

6. Physical

How close do these goals come to the goals you set a little while ago under the Goal Setting heading?

Vitamins For the Mind

Every great man, every successful man, no matter what the field of endeavour, has known the magic that lies in these words: Every adversity has the seed of an equivalent or greater benefit.

W. Clement Stone

People are not disturbed by events, but by their view of events.

Epictetus

Success is not something that can be measured or worn on a watch or hung on the wall. It is not the esteem of colleagues, or the admiration of the community. Success is the certain knowledge that you have become yourself, the person you were meant to be from all time. That should be reward enough.

Dr George Sheehan

No one plans to fail, they simply fail to plan.

Dale Carnegie

Habits change into character.

Ovid

It is difficulties that show what people are.

Epictetus

To believe in the heroic makes heroes.

Disraeli

Power to Choose

Who said it could not be done? And what great victories has he to his credit which qualify him to judge others accurately?

Napoleon Hill

Anyone can carry his burden, however hard, until nightfall. Anyone can do his work, however hard, for one day. Anyone can live sweetly, patiently, loving purely, till the sun goes down. And this is all life really means.

Robert Louis Stevenson

Daring ideas are like chessmen moved forward; they may be beaten, but they may start a winning game.

Goethe

Every problem contains within itself the seeds of its own solution.

Arnold

Fear makes the wolf bigger than he is.

German Proverb

The only time a tortoise makes any progress, is when he sticks his neck out.

Some people drink at the fountain of knowledge — others just gargle.

Suggested Books for Further Reading

I don't think any one author or any one book has all the answers. The process of personal development is an on-going experience, so I encourage you to grow on from here. These books may help:

TITLE	AUTHOR
Your Erroneous Zones	Dyer
Psychocybernetics	Maltz
Pull Your Own Strings	Dyer
A New Guide to Rational Living	Ellis&Harper
The Greatest Miracle in the World	Mandino
The Time Trap	Mackenzie
What do You Really Want for Your Children	Dyer
Why Wasn't I Told	McInnes
Being Happy	Matthews
Getting on With Teenagers	Montgomery,Morris
The Power of Positive Thinking	Peale
I'm OK — You're OK	Harris
How to Win Friends and Influence People	Carnegie
Enthusiasm Makes the Difference	Peale
The Road Less Travelled	Peakc
The Success Factor	Stanton
Anatomy of an Illness	Cousins
Why am I Afraid to Say Who I Am?	Powell

Power to Choose

The Magic of Believing	Bristol
Tough Times Never Last, Tough People Do	Schuller
Three Magic Words	Anderson
Doing it Now	Bliss
Understanding Stress Breakdown	Wilkie
The Plus Factor	Stanton
Lateral Thinking	de Bono
Unlimited Power	Robbins
The Psychology of Winning	Waitley
You Can Do It	Bernard,Hajzler
The Books You Read	Jones
Practical Thinking	de Bono
Swim With the Sharks	Mackay
Getting on With Oldies	Montgomery,Morris
Body Language	Pease
How to Pass Exams	Orr
Goodbye to Guilt	Jampolsky,Hopkins,Thetford
Anger	Ellis
Stress Without Distress	Seyle

Check your book store or library for books on personal development.

HAYDN SARGENT

Haydn Sargent grew up in one of Australia's toughest industrial cities — Wollongong, New South Wales, steel mills territory. And he worked in the steel mills as a youngster during high school holidays and later during college studies, to pay his way.

During National Service in the army, he decided to drop law studies and become a minister. He was a minister in two Housing Commission suburbs in Sydney, a Juvenile Court Chaplain and a Minister in Brisbane in the early sixties.

He started the famous Open Door — Brisbane's first drug counselling service. At this time he commenced working with press, radio and television and his morning radio program was born.

He had lung cancer and knows what it is to fight to stay alive. Doctors called his family to him, twice, to say goodbye. But Haydn Sargent is a positive minded survivor and he returned to his two families — wife Norma and five children and his radio listening family. The rest is history.

Haydn has interviewed thousands of people from Prime Ministers to battlers and the little people he calls 'the backbone of society'. He is part of the daily life of a huge following of people who appreciate his humour, his compassion and his awareness.

He is sought after as a speaker at conferences and functions which need a challenge and a motivator.